DISCARD

JOHN PAUL II

Pope

Biography

JOHN PAUL II
Pope

Alison M. Behnke

A&E

TF
CB

Twenty-First Century Books
Minneapolis

*To my editor, Francesca Di Piazza, who—with equal
parts enthusiasm and reflection—brought her own
knowledge of darkness and light to this work*

Copyright © 2006 by Lerner Publications Company

Twenty-First Century Books
A division of Lerner Publishing Group
241 First Avenue North
Minneapolis, MN 55401 U.S.A.

Website address: www.lernerbooks.com

Library of Congress Cataloging-in-Publication Data

Behnke, Alison.
    Pope John Paul II / by Alison Behnke.
        p.   cm. — (A&E biography)
    Includes bibliographical references and index.
    ISBN-13: 978–0–8225–2798–5 (lib. bdg. : alk. paper)
    ISBN-10: 0–8225–2798–7 (lib. bdg. : alk. paper)
    1. John Paul II, Pope, 1920–2005—Juvenile literature. 2. Popes—
Biography—Juvenile literature. [1. John Paul II, Pope, 1920–2005.
2. Popes.] I. Title. II. Series: Biography.
BX1378.5.B3695 2006
282'.092—dc22   2005045026

Manufactured in the United States of America
1 2 3 4 5 6 – JR – 11 10 09 08 07 06

CONTENTS

Pope John Paul II (left) *prays in 1979 in the cell at the Auschwitz concentration camp in Auschwitz, Poland, where Polish priest Maximilian Kolbe was condemned to die of starvation in World War II. To the pope, Kolbe was an important symbol of holiness.*

INTRODUCTION

On June 7, 1979, Pope John Paul II stood in the prison cell in Auschwitz, Poland—an infamous Nazi death camp. Dressed in his customary creamy white cassock, he stood out in stark relief against the gray, grimy stone walls and floor. In this cell, thirty-eight years earlier, a fellow Polish priest had died for his fellow humans. Maximilian Kolbe had been swept up in a wave of arrests carried out by Germany's Nazi troops as they occupied Poland in World War II (1939–1945). Across the country, Jews, priests, teachers, intellectuals, and others had been seized and sent to death camps such as Auschwitz. Conditions were brutal. But they grew even more dire when ten men were chosen to die by starvation—a punishment for the escape of several other prisoners. One of these men, a young husband and father named Franciszek Gajowniczek, begged desperately for his life. On hearing the man's pleas, Kolbe stepped forward and offered to die in his place. The Nazi captors agreed.

Sixteen excruciating days later, six of the men were dead. The remaining four—including Kolbe—were killed by lethal injection. To Pope John Paul II, this man was the embodiment of priestly sacrifice and holiness—a luminous symbol of faith in the face of utter darkness and evil. He was, John Paul II said, a "saint of the abyss."

Forty years earlier, Pope John Paul II himself had been Karol Wojtyla, a nineteen-year-old university student studying and praying in a tiny basement apartment in Krakow, Poland. Outside his little room, darkness had fallen over his city just as darkness had fallen over his nation. As the shadow of World War II spread across Europe, armed Nazi soldiers patrolled the streets of Krakow, their boots clicking on the cobblestones. As his country was brutally occupied, Karol did not turn to armed resistance. Instead, he turned to the source of strength that Catholic Poles had drawn on for hundreds of years. He turned to God, in the person of Jesus, as taught by the Roman Catholic Church. He believed that history is guided by God and that even a powerless person can help change history by prayer and faith. The Polish Romantic playwrights and poets he eagerly studied taught him that the love of God and love of culture could keep the flame of freedom burning.

At the time, young Karol Wojtyla had no idea what the future held for him. He could not have known that thirty-nine years later, he would become Pope John Paul II, the leader of the Roman Catholic Church. But the young student did know that there was too much to learn for him to slow down, even in the midst of war. God had created a complex world, full of great riches to discover and share, and quick and curious Karol never ceased exploring new ideas and knowledge. He wrote to a friend that first December of the German occupation, saying, "I am very seriously busy. . . . I surround myself with books, I put up fortifications of Art and Learning. I work. Will you believe that I am almost running out of time? I read, write, learn, pray, and fight within myself. Sometimes I feel horrible pressure, sadness, depression, evil. Sometimes I almost glean the dawn, great lightness."

In his lifetime, Karol would witness great personal and historical changes, both joyous and tragic. He would rise from a humble, religious home to become one of the world's most influential leaders. Born and raised in a small, obscure Polish town, he would travel all over the globe. Orphaned and alone at twenty, he would become one of the most recognized people in history. His ideas and policies would be praised—and sometimes opposed—by millions of people. He would see his country divided by oppressive regimes, and he would see it united again in solidarity. He would live through a century, the 1900s, which saw terrible acts of inhumanity, such as the Nazi death camps. He would work and pray that the new millennium in the year 2000 would bring a fresh start for humanity, only to see the world torn by new terrors and wars. And through it all, through the darkest times in his own life and in the world, he would always be led by his belief in Jesus as the light of the world.

Emilia Wojtyla holds her infant son Karol in this 1921 portrait.

Chapter ONE

POLISH BOYHOOD

ON MAY 18, 1920, IN THE SMALL TOWN OF Wadowice, Poland, thirteen-year-old Edmund Wojtyla and his father, Karol, paced nervously in their little apartment. In the bedroom, the midwife was helping Emilia—Edmund's mother and Karol's wife—through her difficult labor. Thirty-six-year-old Emilia had never been physically strong. Her health had worsened after Karol and Emilia's baby daughter, Olga, had died. Now Edmund and Karol hoped and prayed for good news.

At last, the baby was born safely. One story relates that Emilia asked the midwife to open the bedroom window. She wanted the first sound that her child heard to be the choir from Saint Mary's Church across the square, singing hymns.

Emilia and Karol named their baby boy Karol Józef. (Karol is a Polish variation of Charles.) They nicknamed him Lolek.

Karol was born into a country that had just been reborn itself. After a series of wars, Poland had been divided among Austria, Prussia, and Russia in 1795. For more than one hundred years, the Poles had never given up the dream of an independent Poland. After World War I (1914–1918), that dream had become a reality. Karol's father, who had been in the Austrian army, proudly became part of the new Polish army.

Karol was a much loved, healthy baby, with a lively curiosity and a calm temper. His family lived modestly and was liked by their neighbors. Karol Senior, whom most people called the Lieutenant, was a serious but kind man. He was admired for his intelligence and for his sense of responsibility, justice, and honor. Emilia,

Emilia and Karol Senior were married in 1904 in Wadowice, Poland. Karol kept this wedding portrait of his parents with him all his life.

who had been a schoolteacher before marriage, stayed at home to care for her family. However, her fragile health often confined her to bed, and the family helped with the household chores. Although Emilia tried to present a strong front, her family knew that she suffered.

FAMILY AND FAITH

Emilia and the Lieutenant raised their sons in the Roman Catholic religion. Both parents were patriotic and religious, as was common for their time and place. For many Poles, being Catholic was an inseparable part of being Polish. During the years that Poland had not existed as a nation, Catholicism had helped maintain Polish identity and a sense of community. In particular, Polish Catholics had a special love for the Virgin Mary, the mother of Jesus. It was believed that she was the special protector of Poland, and she was sometimes even referred to as the Queen of Poland.

From Karol's first days, he was shaped by Catholic culture. Besides going to church for Mass, the central worship service, Catholics have a rich tradition of religious symbols and rites. The walls of the Wojtyla home were hung with sacred images. A small font near the front door held holy water, blessed by a priest. On Sundays the Lieutenant or Emilia usually read aloud from the Bible. They also taught their sons how to bless themselves with the sign of the cross and how to say the rosary, a series of prayers to God through Mary. Prayer was a daily part of the family's life.

Two-year-old Karol with his parents in 1922. The Lieutenant wears his military uniform.

The Wojtylas were never disrespectful of people who followed other faiths. Six thousand of Wadowice's residents were Catholic, while the rest of the population—another two thousand people—was Jewish. Anti-Semitism (strong prejudice against Jews) was common in Poland. The church had taught over centuries that all Jews were guilty forever for the death of Jesus. But Karol's family was not anti-Semitic. The Wojtylas' apartment was in a house owned by a Jewish family who lived downstairs. Another Jewish family shared the building's second level with the Wojtylas. Karol played with their daughter, Regina.

In 1924 Edmund enrolled in the Jagiellonian University in Krakow. The city, the traditional cultural center of the country, is thirty miles northeast of Wadowice.

Edmund studied medicine there and made his family proud. Four-year-old Karol, who idolized his big brother, missed him greatly.

Karol began school himself in September of 1926. Each day he walked to the nearby public elementary school for boys. Karol was popular with classmates and teachers alike. A well-mannered and obedient boy, he was also a bright student with an active mind. He also loved to be physically active and was very athletic. In the summer, he swam in the town's river, and in the winter, he and his friends skated on the river's ice.

Karol was also a good goalie in soccer. School soccer games were often between Jewish and Catholic teams. If the Jewish team was short a player, Karol would volunteer to play for them. Many Jewish boys attended Karol's school, and Karol had both Jewish and Catholic friends. Behind the school was a synagogue, the Jewish place of worship.

While Karol grew, Emilia's health continued to deteriorate. In about 1927, her husband retired from the army to help take care of her. Living on the Lieutenant's small army pension (retirement pay), the family watched their expenses closely.

On the morning of April 13, 1929, Karol left for school as usual. While he was gone, Emilia, forty-five years old, died of heart and kidney failure. Karol was called home and told the news.

The family was devastated. But people commented on how well Karol handled his mother's death. "It was

This photograph of Karol was taken in 1929, the year his mother died.

God's will," the boy said. Still, her loss left a hole in his life. Following Emilia's funeral, the Lieutenant took Karol and Edmund to the nearby town of Kalwaria Zebrzydowska. Kalwaria, an important pilgrimage site for Polish Catholics, is a shrine dedicated to the Virgin Mary. Karol knelt there before the image of Mary as a mother, holding the baby Jesus. With his father and brother, he prayed for his own mother. He was not quite nine years old.

FATHER AND SON

Edmund soon had to return to his classes, and Karol and his father were left all by themselves. The apartment seemed empty and sad. But the Lieutenant tried hard to give his young son a good home. He had often cooked, cleaned, and cared for his sons as Emilia's health had failed, and he continued these tasks on his own. The Lieutenant had trained to be a tailor before beginning his military career. The ex-officer often mended clothing in the evening as Karol did school-work. He even took apart his old army uniforms to make clothes for his growing son.

The grieving father and son gradually settled into a simple daily routine. To help stave off the loneliness, they put their beds in the same room. The Lieutenant prepared a plain breakfast each morning before send-ing Karol off to school, and at noontime, father and son met for lunch at a restaurant. In the evenings, Karol and his father often went for walks together. They talked of subjects including Polish history and literature, for the Lieutenant had always loved his country and its culture. Sometimes they went to the movie theater or played indoor soccer, kicking a ball across the apartment floor.

In May 1930, Edmund graduated from the univer-sity. He had earned his medical degree with high hon-ors, and the Lieutenant and Karol traveled to Krakow for the occasion. Both were filled with pride, and Karol, impressed by the university's grandeur, dreamed of achieving such success himself. Soon the new doctor found a position at a hospital not far from Wadowice. Karol, thrilled to have his brother closer to home, visited him whenever possible, and Edmund came home on weekends when he could. Wadowice is located in the foothills of the Carpathian Mountains, and the brothers enjoyed long hikes in the beautiful

Altar boys from Saint Mary's Church in Wadowice are pictured here with Father Kazimierz Figlewicz (front row, center) *in 1930. Karol is seated second from left.*

landscape. Edmund also taught Karol to ski, which Karol loved and was good at.

Karol, a promising student, entered Wadowice's high school in 1930. Father Kazimierz Figlewicz, a religion teacher there, described Karol as "a very lively boy, very talented, very quick and very good. He had an optimistic nature though, after a more careful look, one could discern the shadow of early orphanage. . . ."

Like many Catholic boys, Karol became an altar boy around the age of ten or eleven, serving at Saint Mary's during Mass. In addition to his duties on Sundays, he and his father attended morning Mass several days a week. But, while devout, Karol was not thought of as unusually pious. His greatest interests were school, soccer, and friends.

One of his closest companions was Jerzy Kluger, a fellow soccer player. Like many of Karol's schoolmates and friends, Jerzy was Jewish. His father was the leader of the Jewish community in town. Even as Polish anti-Semitism continued to grow, Karol never accepted it, and it never came between the boys. They often studied and played together.

NEW SADNESS

On December 5, 1932, tragedy once again darkened Karol's life. On that wintry day, he learned that his brother was dead. Twenty-six-year-old Edmund had been working day and night, caring for patients with scarlet fever. The dedicated doctor was struck with the deadly disease himself. After several miserable days of fever and pain, he died in one of his own hospital's beds.

Karol was crushed. He had been very close to Edmund, finding happiness in his company and looking up to him as a role model and a friend. "My brother's death," he said, "probably affected me more deeply than my mother's, because of the peculiar circumstances, which were certainly tragic, and because I was more grown up."

After this death of another loved one, he was, as he later recalled, "left alone with my father, a deeply religious man. . . . Sometimes I would wake up during the night and find my father on his knees, just as I would always see him kneeling at the parish church." Following this personal example of "constant prayer," Karol began stealing a few minutes at Saint Mary's in the mornings or briefly leaving the room while studying with friends, to kneel and pray.

TAKING THE STAGE

As Karol's faith deepened, he also investigated new interests. Wadowice had a thriving cultural and intellectual life, because of its closeness to Krakow. Karol's high school had an excellent set of teachers. One of the most popular was Father Edward Zacher, a priest who taught religion and who also had a science degree. He sometimes discussed astronomy and physics with his students.

Karol and his father are pictured here during a trip to Czestochowa in 1936. The two of them found great comfort in each other's company—as well as in their faith—after the death of both Emilia and Edmund.

Father Zacher's lectures fascinated Karol, sparking a lifelong interest in the connection between religion and science. Karol was especially talented in languages, including Latin. Latin was still the language of the Catholic Church, with all Masses held in that language. He became interested in his native Polish language, as well, and he dabbled in writing poetry. Whatever his private sorrows, they didn't affect his schoolwork. Throughout high school, he received very high grades.

When he was about fourteen, Karol found a new passion: the theater. He began acting, proving to be a natural on stage. His father had already introduced him to some of Poland's great poets and playwrights, from the Romantic Era of the 1800s. Karol pored over these masters, including Cyprian Norwid, Juliusz Slowacki, and Adam Mickiewicz. He lost himself in the beauty of their patriotic, romantic words, which helped form his ideas about history and faith. While many European thinkers and writers in the nineteenth century had rejected religion, the Polish writers had embraced it. In their passionate writings, the long suffering of Poland was compared to the suffering of Jesus—a suffering that would, in the end, lead to salvation.

As Karol explored his love for drama, he met Mieczyslaw Kotlarczyk, a young Polish language teacher who was only a few years older than himself. The Kotlarczyk family was very active in Wadowice's theater scene. Their home was a gathering place for local artists, actors, and intellectuals, a forum for

Karol (center) *found the theater to be a natural outlet for his talents. In this 1936 photograph, he poses with two costars of the play* Lancers of Prince Joseph.

ideas and conversation. Karol loved spending time there, and the Kotlarczyks welcomed him into their circle. With their guidance and friendship, Karol soon was not only acting in plays but also planning and directing them.

Karol's other activities included membership in the local arm of the Marian Sodality, a Catholic youth group dedicated to the Virgin Mary. Father Zacher was the group's adult leader, and Karol enjoyed spending more time with the intellectual young priest. Karol eventually was elected president of the sodality's Wadowice branch.

As Karol prepared for graduation in May 1938, some people wondered if he would go to a seminary (a school to prepare for the priesthood). When the archbishop of Krakow, Adam Stefan Sapieha, visited his high school that year, Karol—as the school's best student—was chosen to deliver a greeting. Sapieha asked whether the impressive young man might become a priest. When told that it seemed unlikely, legend has it that the archbishop replied, "A pity."

But Karol had no intentions of pursuing priesthood. He had other loves and interests. "Girls," he said, referring to the Catholic ban on priests marrying, were "not the issue." Instead, he was "completely absorbed by a passion for *literature* . . . and for the *theater*." He was eager to enroll in Jagiellonian University, as Edmund had, and to follow these passions. But, still getting by on the fifty-nine-year-old Lieutenant's pension, the father and son could not afford to live separately. So in August 1938, they packed their bags, said good-bye to Wadowice, and left for Krakow together.

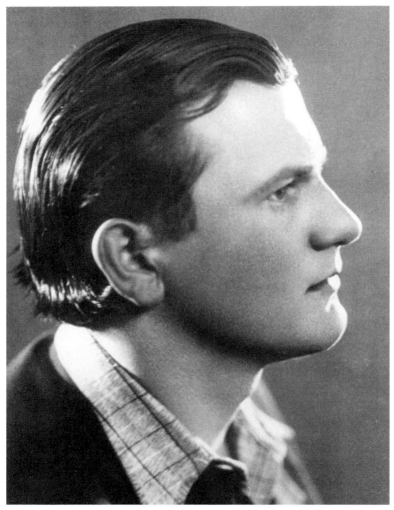

Karol appeared on a poster for Studio 39, a theater in Krakow, Poland. Karol continued to pursue his interest in the theater after he and his father moved to the city.

Chapter **TWO**

WAR YEARS

ARRIVING IN THE HISTORIC CITY OF **K**RAKOW, THE Wojtylas moved into a basement apartment on Tyniecka Street. The apartment was small and dark, but it sat across the street from the Vistula River. It was also within sight of the city's magnificent Wawel Cathedral, presenting eighteen-year-old Karol with a dramatic view each morning.

Karol threw himself into his schooling and other activities. He took courses in Polish literature, Russian, and linguistics (the study of language). He also joined the university's Marian Sodality and continued going to Mass regularly. He soon found theater groups where he pursued his love of drama, as well as student groups where he discussed literature and attended readings. He began writing poetry again and took private French lessons.

All of these activities brought Karol into contact with many new people, and as in Wadowice, he was popular. However, he did not often go to student parties or stay out late at Krakow's pubs. He had women friends, but no romances of note. Some of his acquaintances found him to be friendly but reserved. Juliusz Kydrynski, one of his closest friends, recalled his "gray-blue eyes, which, often thoughtful and serious, reflected nonetheless a deep joy about life." But Juliusz also observed that "with all his sense of humor and his unquestioned social charm, . . . Karol was much more serious than us, a bit closed within himself as if he were always meditating about problems that surpassed us. . . ."

INVASION

As Karol settled into the busy life of a student, rumblings of war sounded in Europe. An aggressive Germany, under the leadership of Adolf Hitler and the Nazi Party, occupied Austria in March 1938 and Czechoslovakia in the fall. On September 1, 1939, the beginning of Karol's second year in Krakow, the rumblings crashed into full-fledged war. The Nazis marched into Poland from three directions, and World War II began.

That first morning of September, Karol attended Mass at Wawel Cathedral. The priest was Father Figlewicz, his old Wadowice teacher, who had moved to Krakow.

As part of his brief military training, Karol (second from right) *helped build this military building in July 1939, just months before the German Nazis marched into Poland, beginning World War II. But as a college student, Karol was exempt from service.*

As the sound of bombs began to tear through the sky overhead, the priest and the student went through the holy rites as if nothing was happening. But Father Figlewicz later recalled, "This first wartime Mass, before the altar of the Crucified Christ and in the middle of the scream of sirens and the thud of explosions, has remained forever in my memory."

ERASING POLAND

By the end of September 1939, Poland had been split into three parts. The Soviet Union, which at this time was Hitler's ally, took over eastern Poland. The German army occupied western Poland. Central Poland became a protectorate (dependent state) also occupied by Germany. For the Polish people, the division of their homeland once again was a terrible tragedy.

The occupation immediately created hardships. Poland's division left family members and friends separated by new borders. Vital food and fuel became difficult to obtain. As Karol wrote to Mieczyslaw Kotlarczyk in Wadowice, daily life "consist[ed] of queues [lines] for bread and of rather rare expeditions for sugar...and of black nostalgia for coal." The Lieutenant's pension was cut off by the Germans.

Much more deeply troubling developments soon emerged. The Nazis were radically anti-Semitic and saw the extermination of all Jews as part of their mission. They rounded up Polish Jews. During the war, millions of Jews in Poland—including those in Wadowice—and throughout Europe would be arrested, forced into segregated neighborhoods called ghettos, sent to concentration camps, and murdered.

Everything close to Karol's heart was affected by the German occupation. Roman Catholicism—a symbol and protector of Polish culture—was a key victim of the Nazis' plans, as they sought to wipe out any possible source of Polish resistance. The Nazis closely monitored or shut down completely churches and religious teaching institutions. They sent thousands of priests, monks, and nuns to the concentration camps. Most religious gatherings were forbidden.

Jagiellonian University was also closed. The Nazis called a meeting of the university faculty. Close to two hundred teachers—almost all the school had—attended. But the meeting was a trap. They were herded onto

THE DARK NIGHT OF POLAND

German plans for Poland were brutal. The Nazis intended to do everything in their power to blot out Polish culture. Hans Frank, the German governor-general based in Krakow, sent orders to his subordinates outlining these plans. They left very little to the imagination.

"The Pole has no rights whatsoever. His only obligation is to obey what we tell him. He must be constantly reminded that his duty is to obey.

"A major goal of our plan is to finish off as speedily as possible all troublemaking politicians, priests, and leaders who fall into our hands. I openly admit that some thousands of so-called important Poles will have to pay with their lives, but you must not allow sympathy for individual cases to deter you in your duty, which is to ensure that the goals of National Socialism [the Nazi Party] triumph and that the Polish nation is never again able to offer resistance.

"Every vestige of Polish culture is to be eliminated. The Poles who seem to have Nordic appearances will be taken to Germany to work in our factories. Children of Nordic appearance will be taken from their parents and raised as German workers. The rest? They will work. They will eat little. And in the end they will die out. There will never again be a Poland."

buses and sent to a concentration camp. Polish intellectuals, students, workers, and religious leaders responded to these attacks as well as they could, founding a range of underground (hidden and illegal) organizations. Some had a military aim, but many were formed simply to keep Poland's arts and culture alive. Teachers who had escaped the first arrests held classes secretly in apartments.

These activities brought great danger. People could be arrested and shot or sent to the camps for the slightest disobedience. Despite the risks, Karol attended classes and met with friends to read Polish plays and to perform them for small audiences in people's apartments. Karol wrote several plays himself, along with many poems. Much of his work during this time focused on biblical stories or themes, such as injustice. He wrote of the importance of holding on to faith and hope during times of trial.

Karol also attended the restricted church services and joined underground Catholic groups that began forming. One was the Living Rosary, a network of youth led by an eccentric tailor named Jan Tyranowski. Karol met Tyranowski in early 1940. Tyranowski was a layperson (someone not officially appointed to religious life) who was an inspiring speaker and an intense Christian mystic.

Mysticism is a spiritual approach to life that encourages a personal relationship with God through prayer and silent meditation. It was not entirely new to Karol, and Tyranowski encouraged him to develop his inner life further along these spiritual lines. He introduced Karol to the writings of Saint John of the Cross, a six-teenth-century Spanish mystic, whose most famous work is entitled *The Dark Night of the Soul.* Karol later described Tyranowski as "one of those unknown saints, hidden like a marvelous light at the bottom of life, a depth where night usually reigns."

LABOR AND LOSS

In September 1940, the Germans put Karol and several friends—including Juliusz Kydrynski—to work at the Zakrzowek limestone quarry, which was about a three-mile walk from the Wojtylas' apartment. Karol worked long days, doing tasks such as breaking up limestone and shoveling the heavy rock into carts. As winter set in, he often labored to exhaustion in the bitter cold. Lunch might be a piece of bread, some beet jam, and a cup of weak coffee. Nevertheless, he was relieved to be earning a small amount of money to support himself and his father.

The job was his first experience as a manual laborer. He came to respect the other workers. He was present when a fellow worker was killed by rocks from a dynamite explosion, and he was left with "a sense of wrong" from that tragedy.

Around Christmastime, the Lieutenant fell ill. With his father confined to bed in the cold little apartment, Karol hurried home each night with food and medicine. On February 18, 1941, Karol headed to the apartment with dinner for his father as usual. Entering the apartment's bedroom, Karol was confronted with the sight of his father's lifeless form on the bed—dead of a heart attack.

At twenty years old, Karol had lost the last remaining member of his immediate family. "I never felt so alone," he would later write. He called a priest to perform the last rites (Catholic rituals for death). For the rest of that long night, he knelt by his father's body, overwhelmed by grief. Guilt at having missed his father's final moments burdened him too. His friend Juliusz stayed with him, and the two prayed and reflected on life and death. Afterward, too sad to stay alone, Karol moved into the Kydrynski home. Their kindness during this bleak time was important to him.

After the loss of the university and then of his father in the midst of war, Karol felt uprooted from his old life. He found meaning and peace in his spiritual life and in solitude with God. But he did not turn away from his old loves. That August his Wadowice friend and mentor Mieczyslaw Kotlarczyk came to Krakow. Mieczyslaw and his family moved into the Wojtyla basement apartment, which still sat empty. Mieczyslaw founded an underground theater group, the Rhapsodic Theater. They performed what they called the "theater of the living word," presenting plays with few props or scenery and risking serious punishment if caught. Karol immersed himself in the theater's activities, and he moved back into the apartment, made bearable by friendship. But, in the back of his mind, the idea that God wanted him to be a priest slowly took root and started to shine like a light.

In October 1941, Karol was transferred to the Solvay chemical plant. The work there was much easier physically. Most of the plant's other employees were lifetime laborers with little education. The young student and his coworkers got along well. Many of the older workers went out of their way to allow him private time to read the books he brought with him or to meditate. The cook sometimes gave Karol—who had grown very thin—an extra-thick slice of bread. Karol's further contact with the world of manual work and the kindnesses and dignity he encountered there made a profound impression on him.

A NEW CALL

In the face of the brutalities of war—fear, poverty, separations, trauma, and death—the priesthood appeared more and more to Karol as a way to serve humanity. As he put it later, "After my father's death, I gradually became aware of my true path. I was working at the factory and devoting myself, as far as the terrors of the occupation allowed, to my taste for literature and drama. My priestly vocation took place in the midst of all that, like an inner fact of absolute clarity. . . ."

Catholics believe that the priesthood is a vocation, or a call from God. Karol kept his growing vocation to the priesthood private, but as time under the occupation dragged on, some of his friends noticed a change in him. Some began to wonder if he might follow a religious calling after all. Then, in the autumn of

1942, Karol—apparently without speaking of it to anyone beforehand—went to confession as usual. (Confession is a rite in which Catholics seek God's
forgiveness for their sins through speaking to a
priest.) But at this confession, he made a very unusual
announcement: his desire to be a priest.

To prepare for the priesthood, Karol had to attend a
seminary. But seminaries had been banned, and anyone
found studying for the priesthood could be arrested or
killed. Nevertheless, underground schools still operated.
In Krakow the secret seminary was run by Archbishop
Sapieha—the visitor who had been impressed with
Karol at Wadowice's high school. Welcoming the news
that Karol was called to the priesthood, Sapieha
accepted him into the seminary. Like the other nine
students in the underground school, Karol would do
most of his work on his own, sometimes meeting individually with a professor in a church or private home.
Because of the dangers, the students were instructed to
tell no one of their decision.

Accordingly, Karol carried on as though nothing had
changed. He continued to work at the Solvay plant
and to take part in Rhapsodic Theater productions,
and he visited his father's grave every day. He did
begin joining Sapieha for Mass in the archbishop's
chapel each morning. But Karol's acquaintances, used
to the sight of him reading, praying, and attending
church, noticed little difference in his behavior.

In the spring of 1943, Karol finally told Mieczyslaw

the news. He needed to devote even more time to studying and could no longer perform with the theater group. Mieczyslaw urged Karol to reconsider. He insisted that the priesthood was not the only way to serve God and that Karol, with his talent, did God's work through the Rhapsodic Theater too. But Karol would not change his mind. His decision to accept God's call was final.

Karol was often joined at morning Mass by another seminarian, Jerzy Zachuta. One morning Jerzy did not come to Mass. Going to his house, Karol learned that he had been arrested by the Gestapo, the German police, the night before. Soon his name appeared on a list of Poles to be shot. Only nine seminarians remained.

Meanwhile, Jews trapped in the ghetto of Warsaw (Poland's capital) were facing unbearable circumstances. Most of the ghetto's original 350,000 inhabitants had been deported to the Treblinka concentration camp. On April 19, 1943, Jewish resistance groups staged a desperate uprising against the German troops. On May 16, the Warsaw Ghetto Uprising was utterly crushed. About 7,000 Jews were shot. The rest, 50,000 men, women, and children, were shipped to the killing center at Treblinka and other camps.

A second Warsaw Uprising took place on August 1, 1944. Underground resistance groups, including Jewish fighters who had escaped the ghetto, attacked German occupation forces.

Determined to prevent similar situations in other cities, Nazi troops swept through Krakow on August 6.

Archbishop Adam Stefan Sapieha taught Karol and other students at an underground seminary school in Krakow.

The day was later known by Poles as Black Sunday. More than eight thousand men and boys were rounded up and taken away to prison or to concentration camps. Karol and the Kotlarczyks, at home in their basement apartment, prayed in terror as German boots thundered across the floor above. Amazingly, the soldiers didn't think to check downstairs. Still frozen by fear, Karol and his friends hidden in the basement heard the door close behind the Germans.

Over the course of the next two months, the Warsaw Uprising would be snuffed out, with 170,000 to 200,000 Poles killed. Most of the city's remaining 650,000 to 700,000 people were sent to concentration camps. Warsaw was left deserted and destroyed.

Archbishop Sapieha feared more than ever for the safety of his pupils. He decided to move the seminarians into the archbishop's residence. Having disappeared from the outside world, the students no longer went to their jobs or any other outside commitments. They devoted themselves completely to their studies. Living in hiding, they wore cassocks, the ankle-length black robes that are the traditional garment of seminarians and priests.

WAR'S END

On the night of January 18, 1945, Soviet troops drove back the Germans and reached the outskirts of Krakow. (The Soviet Union sided against Germany after Germany attacked in 1941.) As the Germans retreated that night, they blew up a bridge. Karol recalled, "I remember that terrible explosion: the blast broke all the windows of the Archbishop's residence." All of Poland was soon in Soviet hands, and Germany surrendered in May. Though the Poles suspected that the Soviets had their own plans to control Poland, the six terrible years of Nazi occupation were over.

In a film still from a Soviet documentary taken during the liberation of Auschwitz in January 1945, Soviet soldiers speak with freed death camp prisoners.

Poland had lost more than six million people by the end of World War II. With a death rate of almost one out of every five people, Poland's loss was at a higher percentage than any other country involved in the struggle. About half of those Poles who died were Jewish. Poland's prewar Jewish population of more than three million had been reduced to fewer than one hundred thousand. In Wadowice the local synagogue and Jewish cemetery had been desecrated and destroyed. Almost all of the town's Jewish residents had been killed, mostly at the infamous camp at Auschwitz, only one hour away. Many of Karol's neighbors and friends had been among the victims. While some Catholics had helped Jews hide or escape to safety, Karol had not—to his regret. He mourned their loss, and he would never forget its injustice.

Life in the scarred nation continued. In Krakow the underground seminary emerged from hiding, and Jagiellonian University reopened. Karol formally entered the university's theology (study of God) department. He was aware that he had been spared much of the direct horror other people had endured. But he felt that their suffering only reinforced the importance of being a priest and serving others in return. He did not pause in his studies. He only added to his activity by becoming a teaching assistant and joining student groups.

Excelling in his classes as usual, Karol passed his final exams with high grades in the spring of 1946.

His seminary studies, begun in hiding as hostile troops patrolled the city, were drawing to a close.

On November 1, 1946, following a month of intense prayer in preparation, Karol was ordained as a priest by Archbishop Sapieha. Writing of his ordination ceremony fifty years later, he said, "I can still remember myself . . . lying prostrate on the floor with arms outstretched in the form of a cross. . . . The one about to receive Holy Orders prostrates himself completely and rests his forehead on the church floor, indicating in this way his *complete willingness to undertake the ministry* being entrusted to him. That rite has deeply marked my priestly life."

The new Father Wojtyla celebrated his first Mass the next day at Wawel Cathedral. He found it a moving experience to be a priest in the cathedral where Polish rulers and poets and saints were buried, a place that was part of spiritual Polish history. And many of his friends were at the first Mass, including members of the Rhapsodic Theater, fellow seminarians, and his old friend Father Figlewicz.

But there was little time to dwell on the turning point. Just two weeks later, twenty-six-year-old Karol boarded a train, embarking on a journey that would take him out of Poland for the first time in his life. Sapieha—who was sure that Karol was bound for great things—had arranged for him to continue his studies immediately. Karol was headed for Rome, Italy—the seat and center of Roman Catholicism.

A portrait of a young Father Wojtyla in the 1940s

Chapter **THREE**

LEARNING
AND TEACHING

IN ROME FATHER WOJTYLA ONCE AGAIN SETTLED INTO life as a student. From his home at the Belgian College, he enjoyed discovering the city. As the ancient capital of the Roman Empire, it held more than 2,500 years of history. And as the seat of Christianity for some nineteen centuries, it offered much to interest a young priest with a passion for learning. "I carried in me the image of Rome from history," he remembered, "from literature and from the entire Christian tradition. For many days, I crisscrossed the city...and I couldn't fully find the image of that Rome I had brought with me. Slowly, slowly, I found it. It came to me especially after touring the catacombs—the Rome of the beginnings of Christianity, the Rome of the

In 1948 Father Wojtyla (back row, far right) *attended Belgian College in Rome.*

Apostles, the Rome of Martyrs, the Rome that exists at the beginnings of the Church and, at the same time, of the great culture that we inherit."

Wojtyla was especially fond of the church Sant'Andrea del Quirinale because it held the relics (artifacts of a saint) of Saint Stanislaw Kostka, the patron saint of Polish youth. Wojtyla often stopped there to pray. And he was not alone in paying tribute to the saint, noting that "among the visitors to his tomb there were many [German] seminarians. . . . At the heart of Christendom, and in the light of the saints, people from different nations would come together, as if to foreshadow, beyond the tragic war which had left such a deep mark on us, a world no longer divided." He saw the church as a way to unite people and bring peace and healing to the world.

NEW HORIZONS

Wojtyla's fellow residents at the Belgian College were students and priests from all over the world, and he enjoyed their company. Several Americans gave him a chance to begin learning English, and he was also picking up Italian. Although the living quarters were simple and not particularly comfortable, Wojtyla didn't mind.

At his school, the Angelicum, a major topic of study was the writings of the thirteenth-century philosopher and theologian Saint Thomas Aquinas. His philosophy captivated Wojtyla. Saint Thomas taught that the truth of things—including the existence of God—can be discovered through the use of the human mind. The mind, however, cannot be forced to accept the truth. Thomas insisted that an individual's mind and conscience must be free—free, even, to come to the wrong conclusion about God. This belief in human freedom to seek the truth—and in each person's duty to try to reach the truth—became a foundation of Wojtyla's own thought.

After passing the exam for his master's degree with flying colors in July 1947, Wojtyla wrote the paper for his doctorate in theology. His subject was Saint John of the Cross, the mystic to whom Tyranowski, now dead, had first introduced him. Wojtyla wrote that although God is infinitely greater than people, the individual believer comes to have a close relationship with God, a relationship rather like two people in love.

That summer of 1947, Sapieha sent Wojtyla on a tour of Belgium, France, and the Netherlands. This trip exposed Wojtyla to various ways of serving people as a priest. In France Wojtyla learned about the worker-priest movement, a controversial new practice that sent priests to work among dockworkers and other laborers. Wojtyla was impressed by the project, which reminded him of his experiences working beside Polish laborers. But some Catholics thought the worker-priests strayed too far from traditional priestly practices, which at that time kept priests separate from laypeople. For instance, when priests celebrated Mass, they did so with their back to the people in the pews. And the Mass was said in Latin, which most laypeople did not understand. Furthermore, the role of the priest was viewed as superior to the lives of laypeople. Wojtyla did not agree with this view. For him, each individual was equally important in the eyes of God and in the church.

Back in Rome in the autumn of 1947, Wojtyla devoted himself to his last year of study. In June 1948, he passed his doctoral exams with high grades, and his finished dissertation—a work of 280 pages, written entirely in Latin—was accepted by the school.

COUNTRY PRIEST, CITY PRIEST

After finishing up at the Angelicum, Wojtyla headed back to Poland. During his absence, he had kept in touch with friends through letters and had worked to "maintain incessantly [his] spiritual contact with the Motherland—through thought, prayer, and reading." But in the years since he had left, Poland, officially called the Polish People's Republic, had undergone dramatic changes. The Soviet powers that had freed the nation from the Germans had stayed on with their own goal of installing a Communist government in Poland. Arriving in Krakow, Wojtyla found a country that had gone from one occupation to another.

"FITTING A SADDLE TO A COW"

Following World War II, the Soviet Union—led by the ruthless dictator Joseph Stalin—worked to install Communist governments in countries throughout Eastern Europe. Communism is a political and social model based on the idea of commonly owned (rather than privately held) property. In a Communist system, the government controls goods and distributes them among citizens. In addition, Communist governments discourage, limit, or ban the practice of religion. Poland, as a very strongly Catholic nation with a long history of struggle against outside powers, did not take easily to the new system. In fact, Stalin himself described the process as being like trying to put a saddle on a cow.

But with thousands of armed Soviet troops in the country and with Soviet-supported Communist officials in high positions, a Communist Polish government was soon in place. Under Communism, the Polish people would again endure periods of great suffering, from food and fuel shortages to the violent suppression of resistance and even the threat of another war. The government imposed censorship on newspapers and radio, and activities of the Catholic Church were limited and closely watched. Tens of thousands of people disappeared into harsh Soviet prison camps in the Soviet Union and elsewhere. Once again, many Catholic clergy were victims. But throughout the hardships, the "cow" stubbornly resisted the saddle that had been forced on it, and the majority of Poles remained firmly—if quietly—anti-Communist.

Within a few weeks, Wojtyla was on his way to the tiny village of Niegowíc. Sapieha—who had been named a cardinal (highly placed official in the Catholic Church)—had assigned him to be an assistant pastor. He would serve the Niegowíc parish, a region that encompassed about one dozen other small villages. The assignment gave Father Wojtyla his first experience with pastoral work (meeting the spiritual needs of a local church community) and exposed him to Poland's humble rural life firsthand. He taught religion in grade schools and performed the normal priestly duties of baptisms, weddings, funerals, celebrating Mass, and hearing confessions. Listening to confessions, Wojtyla realized that this is "where priests encounter people in the depths of their humanity."

Wojtyla soon became a friend as well as a pastor to the local villagers. He began setting up activities for Niegowíc youth, including hikes, plays, and soccer games. He was tireless when it came to visiting houses in the villages—though it could be quite a challenge in the winter. As Wojtyla described it, "Snow will cling to your cassock, then it will thaw out indoors, and freeze again outside, forming a heavy bell around your legs, which gets heavier and heavier, preventing you from taking long strides. By evening, you could hardly drag your legs. But you have to go on, because you know that people wait for you, that they wait all year for this meeting."

In March 1949, Sapieha called Wojtyla back to

Father Wojtyla shaves during a camping trip in the 1950s.

Krakow and assigned him to the parish of Saint Florian. At this new parish, which was made up mostly of university students, the priest worked with and guided young Catholics. Once again, he set about organizing a busy schedule, often working sixteen to eighteen hours a day. Father Wojtyla delivered interesting sermons, played chess, and engaged in late-night conversations on topics from religion to sexuality to jazz music. He could sometimes be found at the movie theater or seeing a play with a group of students. He started a small student choir and arranged excursions into the nearby Polish mountains that he had always loved, leading hikes, kayak trips, and skiing outings. Because the Communist government outlawed priests leading youth groups, Father Wojtyla would not dress as a priest on these outings. He gained the nickname Wujek, or "Uncle"—both to

"Uncle" Wojtyla in his cassock and a young parishioner in 1950

disguise his priesthood from the Communist authorities and out of fondness. Alongside the physical activity of these trips, there was prayer, singing, and discussion, and "Uncle" Wojtyla often held outdoor Mass on a green hillside or beside a river.

The bright and energetic young priest quickly attracted a circle of devoted student parishioners. Some of them began calling their group Rodzinka, or "little family." The friendships formed within this circle were close and lasting. One of the Rodzinka members said, "We felt completely free with him, without any burden. His presence led us to express ourselves. While he was among us, we felt that everything was all right."

FROM STUDENT TO TEACHER

Cardinal Sapieha died on July 23, 1951. Wojtyla mourned the loss of his mentor and the loss of a champion of the Polish church.

Soon afterward, Sapieha's successor, Archbishop Baziak, directed Wojtyla to pursue a second doctorate degree, which would qualify him to become a university professor. Although Wojtyla would have preferred to remain in his current position at Saint Florian's, he followed the archbishop's wishes and began preparing his second doctoral dissertation. This time he chose the German philosopher Max Scheler and the ethics (philosophy of good and bad) of Christianity as his subject.

Scheler's philosophy is about individual people's everyday life experiences. Wojtyla explored how people make everyday decisions about right and wrong and how they could best decide which actions would help them become the person God wanted them to be. He also believed that understanding how to make personal choices for the greater good, rather than for self-serving purposes, was crucial. It could help avoid the sorts of social ideas that had led to Nazism and Communism, which stripped people of freedom and dignity.

Meanwhile, Wojtyla kept up with as many of his student-oriented activities as possible. He stayed in close contact with his Rodzinka and their lives. As many of them began marrying and having children, he performed weddings and baptisms for them.

Father Wojtyla had serious views about marriage and

family. He placed the utmost importance on love. He wrote to a Rodzinka friend, "The ability to love authentically, not great intellectual capacity, constitutes the deepest part of a personality. It is no accident that the greatest commandment is to love." He was impressed with what he saw as a desire for beautiful and pure love in young people. He was always happy to discuss the subject of love fully with them.

Working with young couples, part of what Father Wojtyla taught was that "the sexual drive is a gift from God." He agreed with Catholic teaching that sex between husband and wife should always be open to the creation of new life. Birth control that stood in the way of life was wrong. However, the church did allow "natural family planning." This method is intended to prevent pregnancy by avoiding sexual intercourse during the most fertile part of a woman's monthly cycle. Father Wojtyla taught young couples that while this demanded great control and self-sacrifice, it was what love required.

In October 1953, Wojtyla began leading ethics classes at Jagiellonian University. Many of his pupils were, at first, taken aback by his somewhat shabby dress. He was well known among fellow priests for his extremely simple lifestyle. If people gave him gifts, he gave them away.

But Father Wojtyla's students soon forgot about his threadbare cassock. They found the young professor an absorbing speaker. Wojtyla's ethics centered on the idea of the Law of the Gift: he believed that an individual only becomes a good and whole person through giving of himself or herself to others, rather than pursuing self-interest. Jesus Christ's death on the cross was the ultimate example of self-giving in love, he taught.

Wojtyla's students found him to be a good listener too. "He was interested in us as persons," a former student recalled. He always seemed willing to hear their thoughts. When he disagreed with an idea, he presented his own side clearly, calmly, and usually very persuasively.

Meanwhile, Wojtyla continued to be a prolific and passionate writer. In the space of a few years, he had

In this 1950s photo, Father Wojtyla dons a backpack and sunglasses. His many hikes and camping trips were times for enjoying nature as well as for talking and worshiping with Catholic young people.

written several plays, many poems, and a number of articles and essays. Some of these writings were printed in publications such as *Tygodnik Powszechny* (Universal Weekly), a Catholic newspaper that offered intellectual dissent to Communist rule.

In January 1954, Wojtyla finished his second doctorate. Soon he was given a teaching job in the philosophy department of the Catholic University of Lublin (KUL), about one hundred miles northeast of Krakow. Communist authorities kept student enrollment low and sometimes made it difficult for graduates to get jobs and for faculty to publish. However, the school had the distinction of being the only Catholic teaching institution allowed to operate at all in Soviet-controlled countries.

BIG STEPS

Many things had changed in Father Wojtyla's life since the end of the war just more than a decade earlier. He had gone from a student of theater and philosophy to a priest and from there to a well-respected scholar and teacher. But still bigger changes were ahead. In the summer of 1958, while on a kayaking trip, Wojtyla received a letter instructing him to see Cardinal Stefan Wyszynski in Warsaw as soon as possible. Leaving the trip, he learned that Pope Pius XII had nominated him as auxiliary (assistant) bishop of Krakow. Bishops are priests who are in charge of a diocese (group of parishes). Wojtyla accepted.

On September 28 at Wawel Cathedral, Archbishop Baziak consecrated Wojtyla as a bishop. The church was filled with Wojtyla's many friends and acquaintances, students, and parishioners. Sometime during the long ceremony, a former coworker of Wojtyla's from the Solvay chemical plant called out, using Wojtyla's nickname, "Lolek, don't let anything get you down!"

At the age of thirty-eight, Father Wojtyla had become his nation's youngest bishop. He chose for his motto, "Totus Tuus," Latin for "totally yours," from a prayer addressed to the Virgin Mary.

Five weeks after Wojtyla's consecration, Angelo Roncalli, a man from an Italian peasant background, became the new leader of the Roman Catholic Church. As pope, Roncalli took the name John XXIII. He immediately began to speak of the need to bring the Catholic Church into the modern world—for the church had resisted change for centuries.

Bishop Wojtyla quickly assumed his new duties. He was in charge of the administration of priests and parishes in his diocese. He also ordained new priests. At the same time, he continued teaching at KUL, giving lectures and sermons in Krakow and, as always, organizing outings and trips for youth groups. He saw his role as preacher and teacher. He expanded his visits to more churches outside of Krakow, and he spoke to groups of workers, students, laypeople, and clergy. He always delivered the positive message that God has great love for humanity and confidence in humanity's future.

In January of 1959, Pope John XXIII announced plans for a council, a gathering in Rome of church representatives from all over the world. The Catholic Church holds councils in order to make decisions for the whole church. The preceding council, Vatican I, had been held from 1869 to 1870. Almost one hundred years later, Pope John called for an "aggiornamento," or a bringing up to date, of the church. The council, which would be called the Second Vatican Council, or Vatican II, was scheduled to start in the fall of 1962. The pope asked bishops to send their ideas for agenda topics. Bishop Wojtyla was excited by the prospect of a revitalization of the church. He was one of the first to send his recommendations for items to be discussed to Rome.

In 1960 Wojtyla published his first book, *Love and Responsibility*, on the subject of morals and ethics in relationships and marriage. It reflected his earlier experiences with young people and presented his philosophy that people should not use each other as objects to gain pleasure or power.

CHURCH AND STATE

Since the beginning of Communist rule, the Polish government had tried to control every aspect of people's lives. The church and the government had continuously clashed as state authorities attempted to limit the church's power and influence. Until this point, Wojtyla had not involved himself directly in politics. He believed that Poland would throw off Communism through a gradual process of change, rather than a sudden or violent revolution. However, as bishop he began to challenge the government in small but meaningful ways.

For example, the government frequently refused requests to build new churches. It repeatedly turned down such a request from Nowa Huta, a newly built town for factory workers. In response, Bishop Wojtyla celebrated an outdoor Christmas Mass at an empty field in the churchless town. People flocked to worship, despite bitterly cold weather. Wojtyla also instructed his parishioners not to obey the government's rule that priests be called "Mister" rather than "Father."

While mostly understated, these acts of resistance showed Bishop Wojtyla's determination to stand firm on issues that he felt seriously threatened the strength of his church. And through preaching and teaching, he sought to keep the church tough in the face of the Communist state. The church, in his eyes, was the defender of human dignity in the face of Communism and in the face of a world that Wojtyla saw as increasingly secular (nonreligious).

Catholic religious leaders from all over the world met at the Vatican in 1962 as part of the Second Vatican Council (above). *The council aimed to address the role of the Catholic Church in the modern world.*

Chapter **FOUR**

CLIMBING TO THE HEIGHTS

BY THE EARLY **1960S,** THE NEW DECADE WAS showing itself to be a time of huge social, political, and spiritual changes. Societies were dealing with changing technologies, from the atom bomb to television. People's views were changing, concerning everything from authority to sexuality.

Pope John XXIII had said that it was time to open the windows of the church to the modern world and to trust the guidance of the Holy Spirit in the process. Wojtyla was excited by this openness to change.

On October 5, 1962, Bishop Wojtyla left Krakow for Rome—his first visit since graduating from the Angelicum. He was on his way to the Second Vatican Council.

Vatican II

When Vatican II began, there were more than 900 million Catholics worldwide. Many Catholics had begun to see the Catholic Church as behind the times and even irrelevant to modern life. Many of its practices and policies had remained unchanged for hundreds of years. Yet many church leaders were wary of modernization. They feared weakening church authority. They felt they had to hold firm to traditional morals. Bishop Wojtyla, who wanted the church to be a strong, active force for good in the modern world, was eager to discuss all sides of the issues.

The council's first session opened on October 11, with twenty-five hundred bishops from around the world in attendance. During the session, which was held entirely in Latin, Wojtyla spoke up only twice. When he did, he spoke of his belief that the laypeople, not the clergy, should be the main focus of the church. He listened to the speeches, sometimes writing poetry at the same time. Wojtyla also made several broadcasts over Vatican Radio to keep Polish Catholics informed about the council, a practice that he would continue throughout the council.

Topics discussed at the first two-month session led to significant changes designed to make Mass and other ceremonies more open and accessible to the laypeople. The priest would face the people during Mass, and the Mass began to be said in the language of the people, not Latin. Wojtyla was greatly in favor of these changes.

Pope John XXIII, who had called the Second Vatican Council, died in June 1963.

Pope John XXIII died on June 3, 1963. He had earned the enduring love and affection of Catholics and non-Catholics alike with his warmth, simplicity, and charm. To the relief of many, his successor, Pope Paul VI, declared that the council would continue as planned that autumn.

Vatican II's second session took place between September and December of 1963. Once again, Wojtyla urged the bishops not to underestimate the importance of the people who made up the church. As he put it in his single speech that session, "Every Christian participates in a special, unique, and irreplaceable way in the mission that the Church has received from Christ."

Another important topic was ecumenism, the idea of unifying all Christians—Catholics and Protestants, and the Eastern and Western branches of Christianity—because all shared a faith in Jesus. The Vatican Council stated that the Roman Catholic Church was not the only Christian church, a change from its former belief that it was the only true church.

After the close of the second session, Wojtyla visited the Holy Land (the modern state of Israel). It was his first visit there, and seeing Jerusalem, Bethlehem, and other sites from the life of Jesus had a powerful impact on him. It was a fitting way to close a momentous year.

ARCHBISHOP

But the year was not quite over. When Wojtyla returned to Krakow in late December, his role in the church changed again. Pope Paul VI named him to replace Archbishop Baziak, who had died. On March 8, 1964, in a ceremony at Wawel Cathedral, Wojtyla officially became archbishop of Krakow. The Communist government approved of this appointment because they thought Wojtyla would not be a political threat to them.

Wojtyla moved into the archbishop's residence in Krakow. It was the same building where he had lived as one of Archbishop Sapieha's hidden seminarians. It is a grand building, but never one for luxury, the new archbishop kept his furnishings modest and used only a few of the many rooms.

Archbishop Wojtyla kept his days as full as ever. He packed them with church visits, seminars and retreats, meetings with priests and worshipers, study and reading, and an occasional trip to the mountains. A day never went by without intense prayer. He often prayed face down on the chapel floor, his arms spread out, forming a cross. Visitors found Archbishop Wojtyla to be just as accessible, attentive, and willing to listen to their thoughts as he had ever been.

September 14, 1964, was the first day of the Second Vatican Council's third session. One of the main discussion topics involved the church's place within a changing modern world. Archbishop Wojtyla described the contradictions that both the church and the individual faced. "The modern world," he said, "is new in good and it is new in evil. It contains new values, but also new crises. It is a world of new closeness between people and nations, but, at the same time, a world that is threatening and dangerous in a new way for each person and entire societies. It is a world of progress and luxury, in which the majority of humanity suffers simultaneously from hunger."

The session's most hotly debated subject was religious freedom, arising when a proposal was presented to acknowledge the right of every person to freedom of religion. Some bishops opposed issuing the statement, claiming that it justified teaching and practicing non-Catholic faiths and, therefore, undermined Catholicism itself. However, Wojtyla and many others at the council believed strongly in the God-given right of individual freedom—both in religion and in other areas of life—and felt that it was essential to the basic dignity of every human being. Wojtyla especially condemned anti-Semitism. He wrote the section of the council document *Nostra Aetate* (In Our Time) that said the Jews were not responsible as a group for Jesus' death. This document reversed church teachings that had led to centuries of hostility against Jews.

Once again, Wojtyla followed the session with a pilgrimage to the Holy Land. On returning to Rome, he had his first private audience (meeting) with Pope Paul VI. The pope had been impressed by Wojtyla's speeches and contributions at the council.

The fourth and final session of the Second Vatican Council closed on December 8, 1965. By the time it ended, the bishops and pope had issued a total of sixteen documents stating their views. Wojtyla had contributed to several of them, especially to a declaration on religious freedom, *Dignitatis Humanae* (Of Human Dignity), and a statement on the church in the modern world, *Gaudium et Spes* (Joy and Hope). He considered the work and the entire experience of Vatican II "a great gift to the Church, to all those who took part in it, to the entire human family, and to each of us individually."

The major church reforms that resulted from Vatican II included opening up friendly discussions with other Christian churches and world religions; apologizing for anti-Semitism; and defending religious freedom. The council also emphasized that the church was all the people of God and not just the authorities. Changes in church ceremony made it possible for all Catholics to engage in full and active participation. Another crucial reform was the return to teaching the Bible and not just the catechism, a book of Catholic traditional teachings. The church felt fresh again to many people, although some were saddened at the loss of traditions that followed Vatican II.

The next big event on the archbishop of Krakow's calendar was a very special one to him. In 1966 his homeland would celebrate its Catholic millennium—one thousand years as part of the Catholic Church. The occasion was somewhat troubling to the government, which still tried to limit public religious activity. Nevertheless, a number of observances were allowed to take place during the year. Thousands of Poles made pilgrimages to the city of Czestochowa, home to the Black Madonna—a painting of the Virgin Mary and Jesus that is one of Poland's most beloved symbols.

The Black Madonna from Czestochowa, Poland. The painting is said to have survived many dangers and performed many miracles.

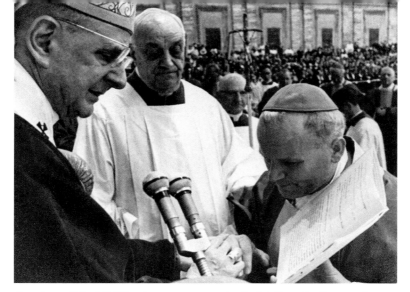

On June 26, 1967, at a ceremony in Saint Peter's Square in Rome, Karol Wojtyla became a cardinal, the second-highest position in the Catholic Church next to the pope.

Archbishop Wojtyla held special Masses in more than fifty churches across the country. And when the government refused to allow Pope Paul VI to visit Poland and deliver a special millennial Mass at the Czestochowa church, Archbishop Wojtyla performed the service in the pope's place.

In April 1967, Wojtyla went to Rome and met with Paul VI. The pope held a high opinion of the archbishop of Krakow. Just two months later, on June 26, 1967, Pope Paul VI consecrated twenty-seven new cardinals. One of them was Karol Wojtyla.

STANDING FIRM

Just as he had as a bishop, Cardinal Wojtyla still insisted on celebrating outdoor Mass at Nowa Huta, while continuing to press for a church to be built there. Finally, the effort paid off. On October 14, 1967, the cardinal attended a groundbreaking ceremony at the future site of the Nowa Huta church.

By fighting for such religious victories, even when they seemed small, Wojtyla saw himself as also fighting for Poles' national identity. He believed that "Polish culture is Christian from its deepest roots. It cannot be torn away from Christianity without destroying it."

The cardinal devoted time to many other issues and activities too. They included his ongoing commitment to the youth of the church; the protection of education—especially of a religious nature—from Communist efforts to limit it; and the support of charity and other expressions of social conscience and justice. Questions of family also still absorbed him, and he formed an institute in Krakow to hold conferences on topics such as marriage preparation, family planning, and child care.

Knowing of Wojtyla's deep interest and strong views on these topics, Paul VI assigned him to a commission (group) writing an encyclical (a letter from a pope to the church's bishops). The encyclical would discuss the church's position on the value of human life regarding family decisions, including abortion and contraception (birth control). Cardinal Wojtyla contributed a great deal to the final encyclical. Much of the document drew on the discussions of an earlier commission founded by Pope John XXIII. However, Pope Paul VI dismissed one of the commission's conclusions: they had concluded that the ban on birth control "could not be supported by reasoned argument." In 1968 Pope Paul VI released the famous and controversial encyclical *Humanae Vitae* (Of Human Life).

Humanae Vitae's main points concerned the life of the unborn, and it restated the church's prohibition of abortion and contraception. The birth control ban was especially controversial, both among church officials and scholars and among average Catholics who felt that the Vatican's leadership did not understand their lives. Liberal theologians and priests, especially in the United States, attacked the teachings on birth control as too rigid. However, Pope Paul VI stood by the document's principles—as did Cardinal Wojtyla.

WHIRLWIND

In August and September 1969, Cardinal Wojtyla traveled to Canada and the United States. He made a special point of visiting cities with large Polish populations. He would venture even farther from home in March 1973, with a journey to Australia for an international meeting of church officials. He stopped in the Philippines and New Guinea on this tour, following that up with trips to Belgium in May and France in November. In 1975 he visited East Germany and also returned to North America, and he headed back to France in 1977. He was committed to spreading the word of Jesus to new places and new generations.

Amid all the travel and the meetings, Wojtyla kept writing and teaching. In December 1969, he had pub-

Cardinal Wojtyla (right) *made many trips to cities around the world. He is photographed here in September 1972 on a trip to Doylestown, Pennsylvania. Doylestown is the home of the Our Lady of Czestochowa national shrine, a sister shrine named after the Polish hometown of the Black Madonna.*

lished *The Acting Person,* a study of human dignity and moral action. In 1972 his book *Foundations of Renewal* was released, analyzing Vatican II and its impact on the church. He also delivered lectures and papers at a variety of conferences and seminars between 1974 and 1978, covering philosophy, religion, family, culture, and other topics.

On August 6, 1978, Pope Paul VI died of a heart attack. Cardinal Wojtyla was saddened by the news. He had regarded Paul VI as one of his role models and friends. However, he had a duty to do, as well. A conclave—a meeting of cardinals to elect the next pope—began on August 25. According to ancient tradition, everything going on within the walls of the conclave must remain utterly secret to the outside world until the cardinals elected a new pope. He

would be chosen from among the cardinals themselves. Each cardinal was assigned a cell—a tiny,
sparsely furnished room. Alone in his cell, Wojtyla
would meditate and pray on the decision before him.

The August conclave turned out to be short. On
August 26, the cardinals elected the kindly, quiet Ital-
ian cardinal Albino Luciani as pope. Luciani became
Pope John Paul I.

But the church was thrown into turmoil by John
Paul I's sudden death from a heart attack on September 28—just thirty-three days after his election.
Wojtyla and the other cardinals hurried back to Rome
in early October for a second conclave.

CONCLAVE

At the previous conclave, the growing divide within
the church between conservative, traditional views
and liberal, modernizing forces had been clear. Looking for a solution, some cardinals began mentioning
Cardinal Wojtyla's name. He had impressed many
with his intelligent, well-expressed views and with his
actions as a tireless priest for the people in his Communist-controlled nation. He was viewed as neither
extremely liberal nor extremely conservative, holding
traditional positions on issues such as family planning, along with progressive ideas on social justice
and individual freedom.

The cardinals were also eager to choose a relatively
young pope in sturdy health. Wojtyla, at fifty-eight years

old, still spent his vacations hiking and skiing in the mountains. While his demanding schedule occasionally took its toll, the athletic cardinal was rarely sick.

In addition, with Rome as the center of the church, Italians had long dominated its history and government, and the last forty-five popes had all been Italian. However, the group of cardinals at this conclave was one of the most international in history. Some felt that this growing church was ready for a non-Italian pope.

Although Wojtyla must have known he was under consideration, he kept his own thoughts private. Once the doors of the Vatican closed behind him and his fellow cardinals, he left his fate in the hands of God.

On October 15, voting began. Outside in Saint Peter's Square, thousands had gathered, eager to learn who the next *papa* (pope) would be. After each vote, they watched for the age-old signal: black smoke from one of the Vatican's chimneys if no pope had been chosen, and white smoke if one had. Seven times, black smoke emerged in the sky over Saint Peter's. Then, on the evening of October 16, 1978, white smoke poured out of the chimney. Cardinal Karol Wojtyla had been chosen pope—the first non-Italian elected in 455 years and the first Polish pope in history.

A newly appointed Pope John Paul II addresses a crowd from the balcony of Saint Peter's Basilica in 1978.

Chapter **FIVE**

THE HOLY FATHER

WHEN ASKED IF HE ACCEPTED THE OFFICE OF POPE, Cardinal Karol Wojtyla was ready with his answer. "In the obedience of faith before Christ my Lord," he replied, "abandoning myself to the Mother of Christ and the Church, and conscious of the great difficulties, I accept." To honor the three popes before him, he chose John Paul II as his name. Then, putting on the all-white cassock of the pontiff, he emerged onto a balcony above Saint Peter's Square for his first appearance as pope.

Most of the throng below had never heard of him, and many were stunned by the fact that their new pope was a Pole. Addressing the crowd in Italian, John Paul II did much to win them over with his first papal address.

Going beyond the usual brief statement to make a personal connection, he said, "Even if I am not sure that I can express myself well in your—our—Italian language, you will correct me if I make a mistake." His Italian, in fact, was fluent. His message of hope in his first address as pope was, "Be not afraid."

POLISH HEART

When word of John Paul II's election reached Poland, people all over the country streamed out into the streets to rejoice. It was a historic moment and a great source of pride for Polish Catholics and non-Catholics alike.

The Communist authorities, on the other hand, saw danger in the news. They expected challenges to the government from the newly powerful Wojtyla. Even the symbolism of a Polish pope, they feared, might threaten Communism's hold over countries with large Catholic populations. For the moment, however, they knew that hostility on their part might lead to unrest or even revolution from within Poland or other Communist-controlled nations. Choosing what seemed to be the safest route, the government made a show of friendliness to the new pope, sending him a letter of congratulations.

On October 23, the pope held a reception for the Polish bishops and a group of Catholic worshipers who had come to Rome for his official investiture (confirmation) as pope the day before. Also at the party was his childhood Jewish friend Jerzy Kluger, who was then living in Rome. Pope John Paul II confessed to his fellow Poles that he felt huge sadness at having to leave his homeland. "It seems," he confessed, "that the human heart—and in particular the Polish heart—is not sufficient to contain such an emotion."

A New Era

Many observers were astonished by how quickly and easily John Paul II took on his new role. He promptly showed the world that, not only was he a natural at the job, he was also a new kind of pope. In the opening months of his papacy, he was a whirlwind of activity. His relative youth and his great energy were immediately apparent as he jumped right into a schedule that would have exhausted most world leaders. His day began at 5:30 A.M. with prayer, followed by Mass, and continued with hours of writing, meetings, and other official business. He held numerous meetings with church officials and world leaders. As he always had, he also took time for walks or other exercise. His personal secretary, Stanislaw Dziwisz, helped manage his time.

The unique qualities of this pope went beyond his physical vigor. John Paul II was less formal in dress, speech, and manner than many of his predecessors. For instance, while popes customarily spoke and wrote using the formal "we" to refer to themselves instead of "I," John Paul II abandoned the practice. Above all, John Paul II was open, friendly, and accessible to the general public. He loved to go into a crowd, hugging, blessing, and touching the people who, as he'd always believed, were the true strength of the church.

John Paul II also proved that he was a master of the modern mass media. Like previous popes, he would issue many written works—releasing his first encyclical within five months of his election—and he would deliver messages on Vatican Radio. The photogenic former actor also was a natural on television, at news conferences, and in photographs. *People* magazine even named him one of the twenty-five most intriguing people of 1978. Soon people all over the world recognized the smiling face of John Paul II.

Yet for all his friendliness and charisma, the new pope was no lightweight when it came to enforcing his view of the church's strict moral code. He described himself, saying, "I am not severe—I am sweet by nature—but I defend the rigidity principle. . . . God is stronger than human weakness and deviations. God will always have the last word." He wasted no time in speaking out on the themes most important to him. These included the consistent defense of life against all threats, including abortion, the death penalty, and euthanasia (mercifully allowing to die or painlessly killing hopelessly sick individuals). He also stood fast by the church's ban on women or married men in the priesthood and took the traditional view that the church's—and the pope's—authority must be obeyed without question. John Paul II thus brought an unusual combination of conservative and liberal views to the papacy.

AROUND THE GLOBE

In January 1979, John Paul II made his first voyage as pope. He traveled in style, with a special plane loaded with more than one hundred crew members, reporters, guards, and other assistants. His first stop was the Caribbean island of the Dominican Republic. After landing in the capital, Santo Domingo, the pope—already proving to be unpredictable—surprised everyone by kneeling and kissing the ground. This dramatic act would become a trademark of his travels. From the Dominican Republic, John Paul II journeyed to Mexico, and then to the Bahamas. In Mexico—a mostly Catholic country—the pope found enormous, adoring crowds waiting for him.

Wherever he went, John Paul II highlighted the topics dearest to him. He spoke of the sanctity of human life, and he pleaded for peace around the world. He also emphasized the importance of individual human dignity—a concept that he also used to address the issues of workers' rights, women's equality, poverty, and religious freedom. These matters were the central themes of his early papacy.

The Latin American trip also presented John Paul II with one of the first political controversies of his papacy. Some Latin American church officials had turned to a movement known as liberation theology. It was based on the idea of using Catholicism to bring about social change. Many people in Latin America suffered from poverty, disease, ignorance, and oppression.

Furthermore, countries such as Nicaragua and El Salvador were in the grip of brutal military regimes. Liberation theology priests and nuns focused their efforts on the poor, sometimes living in the most poverty-stricken communities. They combined Catholic teachings with practical solutions to the people's problems. Liberation theologians were also open to combining religious methods with politics.

John Paul II fully backed the social aims of liberation theology, but he disagreed with its methods, as he saw them. He thought that the movement's political foundation was too close to Marxism, one of the theories behind Communism. Having seen that system's effects on his own Poland, he forbade the practice of liberation theology. He urged Catholics to fight against poverty and oppression with the traditional tools of the church—prayer, education, charity, and patience—rather than political activism. His condemnation of the movement disappointed many Latin American priests, who had hoped that his own experience living under oppression would make him sympathetic to their movement. Priests who would not obey his orders to stay out of politics were often replaced with more obedient priests.

Later that year, Archbishop Oscar Romero of El Salvador, who had supported the aims of liberation theology and had preached for the rights of poor peasants, was assassinated. While saying Mass, he was gunned down by a government-sponsored death squad. John Paul II was appalled, and he condemned the murder, but he did not change his mind about liberation theology.

A more personal trip lay ahead. After months of negotiations, John Paul II went home to Poland as pope for the first time. He emerged from his plane and kissed Warsaw's ground on June 2, 1979, launching nine days of excitement, emotion, and a dizzying blend of patriotism and religion. On that first day, the pope met with government and church leaders, each expressing their desire for harmony. He visited both a cathedral and the presidential palace, and he spoke of Polish history and Polish faith.

Everywhere he went, hundreds of thousands of Poles gathered for a glimpse of their pope. When he reached Krakow—where he had lived for a total of forty years as student, seminarian, priest, bishop, and cardinal—his old hometown welcomed him ecstatically. Outside the archbishop's residence, vast, cheerful crowds lingered late into the night, cheering when he emerged at his window and joined with them in singing Polish songs. From Krakow he made trips to Wadowice, where he visited with old friends, and to Kalwaria Zebrzydowska, where he had prayed with his father and brother after his mother's death. He celebrated Mass in Wawel Cathedral and held a special gathering for young people.

John Paul II also made a solemn visit to Oswiecim-Brzezinka (Auschwitz-Birkenau in German), the site of a World War II concentration camp where four million people, mostly Jews, had been killed. Kneeling on that historic ground, the pope prayed, saying, "I kneel before the inscriptions that come one after another bearing the memory of the victims of Oswiecim." He noted that "the inscription in Hebrew [the traditional Jewish language]... awakens the memory of the people whose sons and daughters were intended for total extermination.... It is not permissible for anyone to pass by this inscription with indifference."

On June 10, the last day of his visit, Pope John Paul II delivered a message of farewell and of hope. "You must be strong, dear brothers and sisters," he told the crowd of more than two million. "When we are strong with the Spirit of God, we are also strong with faith in man.... There is therefore no need to fear."

The energy generated in Poland by the pope's visit had been enormous. The government, aware of the potential for trouble in such a charged environment, had tried to maintain an air of nonhostile authority throughout the nine days. But, while John Paul II was determined to keep the Polish Catholic Church alive and strong, he had stated that the aim of his visit was not to create unrest. He was a Pole coming home to the country and the people he loved.

SOLIDARITY

A year later, in the summer of 1980, the pope's attention was drawn back to Poland. Waves of unrest had swept the country after the government had increased prices

Shipyard workers and members of Solidarity, a Polish trade union, went on strike in August 1980, while supporters stood outside the gates of the shipyard. Pope John Paul II's image, which would become a powerful, internationally recognized symbol for the union, is on display.

for food and other goods. On August 14, nearly seventeen thousand shipyard workers in the port city of Gdansk went on strike in response to the government price hikes and to the firing of a trade union leader. They formed an organizational committee and chose Lech Walesa—a former electrician—as the group's leader.

The workers quickly gained the support of people around the country, and other laborers staged strikes of their own. By September, as the strikes and demonstrations continued to spread, a loose national coalition of workers had formed and become known as Solidarnosc, or Solidarity. Identifying itself with Polish patriotism—and with Polish Catholicism—Solidarity swelled into a powerful movement. Crippled by the widespread strikes, the government agreed to negotiate.

The pope watched these developments closely. The Vatican said little publicly on the subject, although behind-the-scenes communication went on between national leaders including U.S. president Jimmy Carter, Soviet leader Leonid Brezhnev, and the pope himself. When John Paul II did discuss the situation, he stressed his desire for peace and his compassion for the struggles of the Polish people. In January 1981, the pope also showed support for Solidarity by welcoming Lech Walesa and several Solidarity members to an audience at the Vatican.

As usual, however, the pope's busy calendar soon called him away. In February 1981, he left Rome for his first tour of Asia, which took him to Pakistan, the Philippines, Japan, and Guam.

BRUSH WITH DEATH

On May 13, 1981, the pope arrived at Saint Peter's Square in his open vehicle, greeting the gathered people as he did almost every week when he was in Rome. As he smiled and shook hands, the sharp crack of a pistol shot split the air. Struck in the abdomen, the pope crumpled back against his aides. As the crowd seized the fleeing gunman, the critically wounded pope—praying aloud to Mary—was rushed to a Rome hospital where he underwent more than five hours of dangerous surgery. Thousands of people in the stunned audience back at Saint Peter's Square remained there until after midnight, praying and waiting for news.

Bodyguards hold Pope John Paul II seconds after he was critically wounded by a gunman's bullet on May 13, 1981.

The pope's attacker was a young Turkish man named Mehmet Ali Agca. Agca had connections to terrorist organizations, but his reasons for trying to kill the pope were murky.

Within days, the pope was already insisting on holding Mass and meetings at the hospital, and on June 3, he returned to the Vatican. Although he would suffer from his wounds in the coming weeks, his recovery had been remarkable. He had been shot on the anniversary of the famous appearance of the Virgin Mary to children in Fatima, Portugal. He credited his safety to her and reaffirmed his motto, saying, "To you Mary, I say again, 'Totus tuus ego sum': I am totally yours."

Following the incident, the papal vehicle was fitted

with a bulletproof glass enclosure over the back. From then on, the pope—who had so loved being close to the crowd—rode within this safe but strange-looking vehicle, informally dubbed the popemobile.

GLIMMERS OF HOPE

On December 13, 1981, the Communist government— still trying to deal with Solidarity's threat—instituted martial (military) law. Soldiers and tanks patrolled the streets throughout the country. Thousands of Solidarity members, including Walesa, were arrested.

Conditions in Poland worsened as food prices rose again, and censorship tightened. Most travel was restricted. Solidarity was outlawed in October 1982, and even saying its name became illegal. While the movement remained alive underground, it was weakened. Martial law was suspended, although not completely lifted, in early 1983, but daily life remained grim.

Feeling that his people were badly in need of hope, John Paul II had been pressing the government for nearly a year to allow him a second visit. The authorities finally agreed to a trip in June 1983. Speaking to a crowd in Czestochowa, John Paul II made a statement of support and defiance by addressing the importance of the "fundamental solidarity between human beings"—thus uttering the name of the forbidden movement.

As John Paul II left Poland in 1983, changes were gradually on their way. Martial law formally ended in

July, and in October Walesa won the Nobel Peace Prize. Then, in 1985, Mikhail Gorbachev took power in the Soviet Union. The new leader introduced ideas of perestroika (restructuring) and glasnost (openness), marking a dramatic shift in Soviet policies. This shift would extend to the Eastern European nations under Soviet influence, bringing new hope to Poles.

By the time John Paul II returned to Poland for a third visit, in June 1987, Solidarity was operating openly again. Dramatic changes followed the pope's departure. Solidarity gained official status as a trade union, and the increasingly weakened government agreed to negotiate. In 1989 talks culminated in the nation's first post-Communist government, led by Solidarity members. In 1990 Lech Walesa was elected president of Poland.

Following Poland's transition to democracy, a string of nonviolent movements in other Eastern European nations—and finally in the Soviet Union itself—replaced their Communist governments with democracies. Historians have debated how important John Paul II was to this process. Some believe that his 1979 papal visit to Poland helped spark Solidarity, leading inevitably to the collapse of Communism throughout the region. Others think that this view exaggerates his direct influence. But what mattered most to the pope himself was that for the first time in more than fifty years his beloved Poland was truly free.

In March 1983, John Paul II (second from left) *listened to Daniel Ortega, a leader of the Sandinista National Liberation Front in Managua, Nicaragua. In the hopes of promoting peace, the pope visited many such countries as Nicaragua whose citizens endured government oppression and civil war.*

Chapter **SIX**

UNSHAKABLE CONVICTIONS

WITH **POLAND FINALLY FREE AND DEMOCRATIC,**
John Paul II had seen one important battle won. But
most of the problems and issues that he had
addressed since the beginning of his papacy remained.
Pope John Paul II would continue to devote his time
and energy to these issues. His sharp and curious
mind sought solutions and alternative approaches
through many channels, but he always kept the
church's fundamental teachings and moral laws as the
guiding light at the heart of his search.

PEACE FOR ALL

One of the pope's most passionate missions had
always been the quest for peace. That mission had

grown in urgency throughout the 1980s, especially in the Middle East, where violence had escalated throughout the decade. The pope had called repeatedly for an end to a devastating civil war in Lebanon. He also spoke out on the urgent need to find peaceful solutions in Israel. Founded in 1948 as a homeland for Jews, the State of Israel was created out of land formerly inhabited by the Palestinian people. Tensions between Israelis and Palestinians had been a source of conflict ever since. In the 1980s, the conflict had taken the form of terrorism. Pope John Paul II made an effort to hear both sides, holding separate audiences with both Palestinian leader Yasser Arafat and with Israeli prime ministers, including Shimon Peres. His meetings with Arafat—who was widely seen as personally supporting terrorism—were criticized by many observers. But many of the pope's meetings with world leaders would spark controversy, as he met with presidents, prime ministers, monarchs, and even dictators. While condemning violence and injustice, he also believed firmly in the importance of dialogue to reaching any solutions.

Wars also raged in Central and South America. In countries including Nicaragua, El Salvador, Guatemala, and Colombia, resistance movements against oppressive governments pitted rebels and army forces against each other in civil wars. Many of these conflicts dragged on, in various degrees of intensity, for years. John Paul II visited Latin America

In December 1983, Pope John Paul II met with his attempted assasin, Mehmet Ali Agca, to offer his forgiveness.

several times during the 1980s. He generally chose not to take political positions in public but instead to encourage and support the church during troubled times.

Pope John Paul II had made a much more personal act of reconciliation in December 1983, when he paid a visit to his attacker, Agca, in his prison cell. After the pope celebrated Mass at the Rome prison, he and Agca spent twenty minutes in private conversation, during which the pope offered Agca his forgiveness for the shooting.

Meanwhile, John Paul II looked for other ways to address the issue of world peace. Always having had great faith in the power of prayer, he organized the First World Day of Prayer for Peace. It was held in October 1986, in Assisi, Italy, where Saint Francis had lived and worked centuries earlier for peace through faith. The event brought together representatives of

Pope John Paul II (center in white) *was joined by representatives from twelve different religions, including the Dalai Lama, to celebrate the First World Day of Prayer for Peace in October 1986.*

many nationalities and religions in an unusual effort to soothe worldwide war and violence.

THE MEANING OF LIFE

The United Nations named 1994 the International Year of the Family, proclaiming it as an opportunity to "increase awareness of family issues . . . [and] to highlight the importance of families." For Pope John Paul II, this returned his focus to one of the topics that had always been dearest to him—and renewed the controversy surrounding his views on matters of the family, especially abortion and birth control. Although general opposition to these views grew, the pope's own stance never wavered. He explained that the tragedies of Nazism and Communist oppression had shaped the first years of his priesthood and, he wrote, "so it is easy to understand my deep concern for the dignity of every human person and the need to respect human rights, beginning with the right to life. . . . These concerns . . . developed precisely as a result of those tragic circumstances."

In keeping with these concerns, the pope condemned abortion under all circumstances. In 1994 he wrote, "The *legalization of the termination of pregnancy* is none other than the authorization given to an adult . . . to take the lives of children yet unborn and thus incapable of defending themselves. . . . *It is not possible to speak of the right to choose when a clear moral evil is involved,* when what is at stake is the commandment *Do not kill!*"

The pope also maintained the ban on birth control. Many people saw the ban as socially irresponsible in light of a new and devastating disease. Since the early 1980s, HIV/AIDS had become the most pressing health issue of the late twentieth century. With no known cure or vaccination, condoms offer one of the

A demonstrator opposes John Paul II's stance on abortion during one of his visits to the United States in the 1990s.

few forms of protection against the disease. Human rights and health groups urged the pope to reconsider the ban, arguing that access to condoms in disease-ravaged nations could save thousands of lives every year. For example, some of the regions hardest hit by the AIDS epidemic are in Africa, Latin America, and the Caribbean. The church runs many aid organizations in these regions, but church members are forbidden to distribute birth control. But the pope insisted that other solutions must be found, such as promoting faithful, monogamous marriage.

John Paul II saw great evil in what he called a "culture of death." Euthanasia (often known as mercy killing and which the pope called "false mercy"), the death penalty, and drug dealing were all, in his opinion, signs of a growing disregard for the value of human life. He felt that this loss of the sense of the sacredness of life was strongest in the United States and other wealthy nations. He spoke against "unbridled capitalism which puts the quest for power and profit . . . above all other considerations." Such a culture, he argued, viewed people as objects, to be used for pleasure or profit, something he had warned against from his earliest days as a priest.

By the mid-1990s, observers around the world were concerned about the pope's health. They noticed signs that the pope might be suffering from Parkinson's disease, an illness that attacks the central nervous system and affects muscle control. Visible symptoms of

Parkinson's include a stooped or shuffling walk, stiff facial muscles, and trembling of the hands or head. The pope seemed to show several of these symptoms.

WOMEN AND THE CHURCH

Issues around sexuality and gender have remained sources of tension and division in the church. For instance, the pope's position on birth control was related, some people felt, to his views on women and feminism, which were every bit as controversial. Some saw the pope's rigid moral teachings as unrealistic. International woman's rights groups pointed out that many women in developing nations were without access to birth control and often belonged to societies that gave them few rights. As a result, many had no reliable way to protect themselves from AIDS and other diseases, and many faced multiple pregnancies despite health risks or poverty. These groups believed that education and access to birth control were among the most effective ways to help these women improve the quality of their lives. But the pope saw the solution in strengthening the social equality of women and not in changing what he saw as unchangeable moral truths regarding these issues.

He also refused to consider opening the priesthood to women. Other Christian denominations had begun to ordain women, and some faithful Catholic women began to state that they, too, were called to the priesthood. Despite these changes and despite suggestions that allowing women to be priests could stop the alarming decline in the number of new priests, John Paul II stood by the church's tradition of male-only clergy. This teaching is based on an interpretation of the fact that Jesus had only chosen men as his apostles (followers assigned the task of spreading the faith). Some Catholic theologians point out that this is an overly literal and narrow interpretation of Jesus and faith. In a letter on the matter, the pope acknowledged that "the presence and the role of women in the life and mission of the Church . . . remain absolutely necessary and irreplaceable." Nevertheless, he stated without room for argument that "the Church has no authority whatsoever to confer priestly ordination on women and that this judgment is to be definitively held by all the Church's faithful." He ordered that the matter was not even to be discussed.

Yet, at the same time, John Paul II repeatedly pledged his deep respect and reverence for women. For example, in his June 1995 "Letter to Women," he thanked them for their contributions to modern life. He spoke of his "admiration for those women of good will who have devoted their lives to defending the dignity of womanhood by fighting for their basic social, economic, and political rights." Some women, however, felt that the pope's actions spoke louder than his words.

JUBILEE

In November 1996, Pope John Paul celebrated the fiftieth anniversary of his ordination as a priest. He published a book, *Gift and Mystery*, reflecting on his calling and his pastoral career. *"I let myself be freely carried along by a wave of memories,"* he wrote. Carried along by hope for the future, as well, that same month, he also launched preparations for a Holy Year of Jubilee to take place in 2000.

Jubilees are an ancient tradition in the Catholic Church. They are held as times of special worship, celebration, and expressions of justice and forgiveness. This one, known as the Great Jubilee, would mark the two thousandth anniversary of Jesus' birth. The Vatican and all of Rome began getting ready early. Special trips, celebrations, and events were planned, and monuments were cleaned and renovated.

For John Paul II, this jubilee—coming at the end of such a violent century—had a special urgency to it. The jubilee was to be a time for the examination of conscience for each person and for the church as a whole. Preparing for the dawn of the third millennium, the pope wrote, "The Church cannot cross the threshold of the new millennium without encouraging her children to purify themselves through repentance of past errors."

By the opening of the Great Jubilee year, the pope's health had declined considerably, and many observers were concerned for his welfare. Rumors and speculation about his condition began to swirl in the media. Nevertheless, John Paul II achieved his dream of making a jubilee year pilgrimage to the Holy Land. It was an emotional journey for him and included historic

Pope John Paul II stands alone in prayer at the Western Wall in Jerusalem in 2000.

moments. For example, he became the first pope to pray at the Western Wall in Jerusalem, the holiest site in Judaism. While there, the pope followed the age-old tradition of placing a written prayer in one of the wall's many cracks. The prayer read, "God of our fathers, you chose Abraham and his descendants [Jews] to bring your Name to the nations: we are saddened by the behavior of those who in the course of history have caused these children of yours to suffer, and asking your forgiveness we wish to commit ourselves to genuine brotherhood with the people of the Covenant. We ask this through Christ our Lord."

This act, while historic for the Catholic Church, was not so surprising from a pope who had grown up with Jewish friends and neighbors, only to witness the horrors of the Holocaust in his own country. It was not without precedent in his own papacy either. In 1986 he had visited Rome's synagogue, making him the first pope ever to enter a synagogue. In fact, the pope's ongoing outreach to the Jewish community and his drive to make amends for the Catholic Church's past treatment of the Jews was seen by many as one of the most unique and most important elements of his papacy.

In a record-breakingly hot August of the jubilee year, two million people from around the world gathered in Rome for World Youth Day. On the evening of August 19, John Paul II addressed the huge crowd of young people. Reflecting on the disturbing history of the

John Paul II continued to take an interest in involving youth in Catholicism. In August 2000, he welcomed thousands of young people at the opening ceremony of the World Youth Day celebration, a six-day festival held in Rome.

century, he offered inspiration for the future: "In the course of the century now past, young people like you were summoned to huge gatherings to learn the ways of hatred; they were sent to fight against one another. Today you have come together to declare that in the new century you will not let yourselves be made into tools of violence and destruction. You will not resign yourselves to a world where other people die of hunger, remain illiterate, and have no hope. In saying 'yes' to Christ, you say 'yes' to all your noblest ideals."

THE AGING PONTIFF

The beginning of the twenty-first century did not prove itself to be any less violent and destructive than the twentieth century, as John Paul II had longed for. One distressing sorrow as he aged was the continuing cycle of violence in the Middle East and beyond. He continued to plead for peace in the Holy Land and the world.

John Paul II made history again when, at the age of eighty-one, he traveled to Syria in May 2001 and became the first pope to visit a mosque (Islamic place of worship). He pleaded for peace and forgiveness between Christians and Muslims. On that same trip, he visited Greece, where he spoke of healing the rift between the Catholic Church and the Eastern Orthodox Church (the branch of Christianity followed by many Greeks). He never ceased calling for greater Christian unity, and the ongoing divisions between Christian faiths were a great disappointment to him.

The world saw a new kind of terror on September 11, 2001, when devastating terrorist attacks struck New York City and Washington, D.C. The pope expressed his grief for the people of the United States and held another World Day of Prayer for Peace in Assisi. One year later, he recalled the tragedy, saying, "On this sad anniversary, we address our prayer to God so that love may supplant hatred and, through the dedication of all persons of goodwill, harmony and solidarity may be affirmed in every corner of the globe." He added, "Violence can only lead to further hatred and destruction. It can never lead to correct solutions."

In keeping with this belief that violence offers no lasting solution, the pope spoke out against a U.S.-led war against Iraq in early 2003. Though the Catholic Church does hold the Just War Doctrine, teaching that war may be just under certain conditions—including when it is the absolute last resort in the face of an attacker—the war against Iraq was not considered to meet such conditions.

A more personal development for the pope came in May 2003, when the Vatican confirmed that he had Parkinson's disease. Although the battle with the illness had visibly ravaged his body, most observers believed his mind was still as clear and active as ever. Nevertheless, his worsening physical condition raised questions of who might succeed him after his death.

In October 2003, Pope John Paul II celebrated twenty-five years as the Catholic Church's Holy

Parkinson's disease eventually made walking too difficult for John Paul II, so he got around in a specially designed wheelchair.

Father—the silver anniversary of his election. Speaking on the occasion, John Paul II told the audience, "As I thank God . . . for these 25 years totally steeped in his mercy, I feel a special need to express my gratitude to you too, brothers and sisters of Rome and of the whole world. . . . How much kindness and concern, how many signs of communion have surrounded me each day. May the good Lord reward everyone generously! I implore you, dear brothers and sisters, do not stop your great work of love. . . ."

LEGACY

Pope John Paul II's views were often controversial, at times bitterly dividing Catholics. He was modern and traditional at the same time, with his stances on key issues seeming to range from socially progressive to conservative. He spoke of the dignity of individuals while,

MAKING HISTORY

Pope John Paul II lived a long and remarkable life, and his time as pontiff of the Roman Catholic Church held many landmarks. A few of his accomplishments follow.

- He canonized (declared as saints) more than 450 people—more than all the popes of the past four centuries combined.

- He completed more than 100 trips abroad, visiting more than 120 nations and logging more than 740,000 miles.

- He delivered more than 3,000 speeches, in front of many millions of people.

- He was the first pope to have a website.

- He was the first pope to publish several best-selling books and to release a CD. *Abbà Pater,* a recording of John Paul II's words accompanied by music, became an international hit in 1999.

- In 2000 he became the first to star in his own comic book, when *Karol Wojtyla: Pope of the Third Millenium* hit Italy's newsstands. Approved by the Vatican, the comic tells kids the story of the pope's life from childhood, showing him as a skiing, soccer-playing kid himself.

some felt, he ignored certain rights of women and other groups. He also spoke against homosexuality and was firmly opposed to allowing gays and lesbians to marry.

Another controversy arose when allegations and lawsuits erupted over the sexual abuse of children by Catholic clergy, especially in the United States. Some people were upset that John Paul II did not take a stronger stance on the issue. While he condemned such acts, he considered the problem to be primarily an American one rather than an issue for the Catholic Church as a whole.

At the same time, John Paul II was one of the most beloved and most recognized humans on the planet. Millions of people traveled thousands of miles or waited hours for a moment in his presence. Many spoke of his warmth, serenity, and powerful charisma. And supporters and critics alike praised good work that he had done for peace and human rights.

In many ways, these seeming contradictions defined John Paul II as the pope of the twentieth century—just as the twentieth century defined him. It was a century that saw unprecedented war, the horror of the Holocaust, and the oppression of Communism. It also saw great advancement in science, technology, and medicine, even as poverty and deprivation increased. Momentous struggles—and successes—for political and personal rights stood out in harsh contrast to devastating terrorist conflicts in the Middle East and beyond.

In early 2005, the world watched as the pope grew ever frailer. In February he underwent emergency surgery on his windpipe to help him breathe, and the operation left him with difficulty speaking. His public appearances grew less and less frequent, and worried observers began to speculate on the future of the church's leadership. Then, on Easter Sunday, the pope managed to make an

Millions of people from all over the world came to Rome to say good-bye to Pope John Paul II. His funeral was held on April 8, 2005, in Saint Peter's Square in Rome.

appearance to the thousands of worshipers gathered in Saint Peter's Square below his window. For the pope and for all Christians, this holiday is the most important of the year, representing Jesus as the resurrected light of the world. Pope John Paul II struggled to speak. But his body failed him, and he was unable to make his usual Easter address. However, he was able to make the sign of the cross, as his parents had taught him as a boy, once again blessing the crowds below.

Soon afterward, the pope's health worsened dramatically. In his native land of Poland and around the globe—from Mexico to Ireland to India—Catholics and others waited for news. A church official announced that the end was near, saying, "This evening or this night, Christ opens the door to the Pope." And as thousands kept a vigil outside, candles lighting the dark square, John Paul II died at the Vatican on April 2, 2005.

PRONUNCIATION GUIDE

Czestochowa:	chehns-toh-HOH-vah
Karol:	KAH-rehl
Kotlarczyk:	koht-LAHR-chihk
Krakow:	KRAH-koov
Oswiecim:	ohs-VEE-chihm
Sapieha:	sah-PEE-hah
Stanislaw:	STAN-ihs-wahv
Tyranowski:	teer-ahn-OHV-skee
Wadowice:	vahd-oh-VEE-chay
Walesa:	vah-WEHN-sah
Wawel:	VAH-vehl
Wojtyla:	voh-TEE-yah
Wyszynski:	vih-SHIHN-skee

GLOSSARY

altar boy: a boy who helps a priest serve Mass

anti-Semitism: severe prejudice and discrimination against Jews

archbishop: a bishop who administers a group of parishes

bishop: the highest order of ordination in the Catholic Church. Bishops are priests who administer the churches in a local area (diocese).

cardinal: a bishop who administers an archdiocese (group of dioceses). A group of cardinals called the college of cardinals are the chief administrators of the Catholic Church and elect new popes.

clergy: a group ordained to perform sacred functions. The Catholic clergy is made up of unmarried men ordained to be deacons, priests, and bishops.

Communism: a political and economic model based on the idea of common, rather than private, property. In a Communist system, the government controls all goods and money. Communist governments are also usually opposed to religion.

confession: a Catholic ritual in which a person confesses his or her sins to God through a priest and receives God's forgiveness

council: in the Catholic Church, a worldwide gathering of bishops called by the pope to set policy and make decisions for the church

ethics: philosophy of behavior for individuals and groups dealing with what is good and bad

Holocaust: the killing of six million Jews by the Nazis in World War II

Jesus: A Hebrew name meaning "God saves." Christians believe Jesus is the Son of God born of the Virgin Mary.

Mass: the worship service of the Roman Catholic Church

morals: principles about good or bad actions

ordination: the ritual to officially make a person a clergy member (deacon, priest, or bishop)

pope: the head of the Roman Catholic Church, elected by cardinals

priest: an ordained member of the Catholic Church, authorized to perform the sacred rites

seminary: a school to prepare men for the priesthood

sign of the cross: a sign made to connect oneself with the spiritual experience of Jesus' death and resurrection

Solidarity: a Polish anti-Communist movement led by Lech Walesa in the 1980s. Solidarity was comprised largely of trade unions and workers.

Vatican: the physical headquarters of the pope, as well as the papal government, in Rome

Vatican II: the Second Vatican Council, a series of meetings held between 1962 and 1965 to discuss and make decisions about the position of the Roman Catholic Church in the modern world

vocation: from the Latin *vocare,* meaning "call." Catholics believe the priesthood and other spiritual paths are a vocation, or call from God.

SOURCES

7   John Paul II, *Gift and Mystery* (New York: Doubleday, 1996), 37.

9   Tad Szulc, *Pope John Paul II: The Biography* (New York: Scribner, 1995), 109.

18 Ibid., 73.

19 Carl Bernstein and Marco Politi, *His Holiness: John Paul II and the Hidden History of Our Time* (New York: Doubleday, 1996), 27.

19 John Paul II, *Gift and Mystery*, 20.

19 George Weigel, *Witness to Hope: The Biography of Pope John Paul II* (New York: HarperCollins, 1999), 30.

23 John Paul II, *Gift and Mystery*, 5.

23 Ibid., 5–6.

26 Szulc, *Pope John Paul II: The Biography*, 89–90.

27 Ibid., 100.

28 Ibid., 107.

29 Weigel, *Witness to Hope*, 51.

31 Bernstein and Politi, *His Holiness*, 52.

31 John Paul II, *Gift and Mystery*, 10.

32 Weigel, *Witness to Hope*, 68.

33 Virgilio Levi and Christine Allison, *John Paul II: A Tribute in Words and Pictures* (New York: William Morrow & Co., 1999), 43.

37 John Paul II, *Gift and Mystery*, 13.

39 Ibid., 43–45.

41–42 Szulc, *Pope John Paul II: The Biography*, 140.

42 John Paul II, *Gift and Mystery*, 53.

44 Szulc, *Pope John Paul II: The Biography*, 149.

46 Weigel, *Witness to Hope*, 92.

46 Szulc, *Pope John Paul II: The Biography*, 160.

48 Weigel, *Witness to Hope*, 105.

50 Ibid., 101.

50 Ibid., 97.

51 Ibid., 136.

53   Ibid., 150.
59   Bernstein and Politi, *His Holiness*, 96.
61   Szulc, *Pope John Paul II: The Biography*, 232.
62   John Paul II, *Crossing the Threshold of Hope*, trans. Jenny
        McPhee and Martha McPhee (New York: Alfred A.
        Knopf, 1994), 157.
65   Szulc, *Pope John Paul II: The Biography*, 34.
65–66   Robert Sullivan and others, *Pope John Paul II: A Tribute*
        (Boston: Bulfinch Press, 1999), 61.
71   John Paul II, "Twentieth Anniversary of Pontificate, John
        Paul II: Homily," *The Holy See—The Holy Father—John
        Paul II*, October 18, 1998, http://www.vatican.va/holy
        _father/john_paul_ii/homilies/1998/documents/hf_jp-ii
        _hom_18101998_20-Pontificate_en.html (April 6, 2005).
72   Sullivan and others, *Pope John Paul II: A Tribute*, 75.
72   John Paul II, *Crossing the Threshold of Hope*, 218.
73   Weigel, *Witness to Hope*, 269.
73   Ibid., 274.
74   Szulc, *Pope John Paul II: The Biography*, 23.
78   Weigel, *Witness to Hope*, 315.
78   Ibid., 319.
81   Helen Whitney, *John Paul II: The Millennial Pope*, VHS
        (Burbank, CA: Warner Home Video, 1999).
82   Weigel, *Witness to Hope*, 462.
88   United Nations Division for Social Policy and
        Development, "IYF Objectives," *International Year of the
        Family*, n.d., http://www.un.org/esa/socdev/family/IntObs/
        IYF/obj.html (April 6, 2005).
88–89   John Paul II, *Gift and Mystery*, 67.
89   John Paul II, *Crossing the Threshold of Hope*, 205.
90   Whitney, *John Paul II: The Millennial Pope. [text says PBS]*
90   John Paul II, "Colloquium on 'Capitalism and Ethics,'"
        The Holy See—The Holy Father—John Paul II, January
        14, 1992, http://www.vatican.va/holy_father/john_paul_ii/
        speeches/1992/documents/hf_jp-ii_spe_19920114
        _capitalism-ethics_en.html (April 6, 2005).

92   John Paul II, "Ordinatio Sacerdotalis," *The Holy See—The Holy Father—John Paul II*, May 22, 1994, http://www .vatican.va/holy_father/john_paul_ii/apost_letters/ documents/hf_jp-ii_apl_22051994_ordinatio-sacerdotalis _en.html (April 6, 2005).

92   John Paul II, "Letter to Women," *The Holy See—The Holy Father—John Paul II*, 1995, http://www.vatican.va/holy _father/john_paul_ii/letters/documents/hf_jp-ii_let _29061995_women_en.html (April 6, 2005).

93   John Paul II, *Gift and Mystery*, 2.

93   Francesca Di Piazza, "Walking the Walk: A Jubilee Pilgrimage to Rome," *Basilica*, Christmas 2000, 11.

94   John Paul II, "Prayer of the Holy Father at the Western Wall," *The Holy See—The Holy Father—John Paul II*, March 26, 2000, http://www.vatican.va/holy_father/ john_paul_ii/travels/documents/hf_jp-ii_spe_20000326 _jerusalem-prayer_en.html (April 6, 2005).

96   Di Piazza, "Walking the Walk," 12.

97   John Paul II, "General Audience—September 11, 2002," *The Holy See—The Holy Father—John Paul II*, September 11, 2002, http://www.vatican.va/holy_father/ john_paul_ii/audiences/2002/documents/hf_jp-ii_aud _20020911_ en.html (April 6, 2005).

98   John Paul II, "XXV Anniversary of the Pontificate: Homily of His Holiness John Paul II," *The Holy See—The Holy Father—John Paul II*, October 16, 2003, http://www .vatican.va/holy_father/john_paul_ii/homilies/2003/ documents/hf_jp-ii_hom_20031016_xxv-pontificate_en.html (April 6, 2005).

101   "End Draws Closer for Ailing Pope," *BBC News*, April 2, 2005, http://newswww.bbc.net.uk/1/hi/world/europe/ 4402323.stm (April 6, 2005).

SELECTED BIBLIOGRAPHY

Bernstein, Carl, and Marco Politi. *His Holiness: John Paul II and the Hidden History of Our Time*. New York: Doubleday, 1996.

Flynn, Ray, Robin Moore, and Jim Vrabel. *John Paul II: A Personal Portrait of the Pope and the Man*. New York: St. Martin's Press, 2001.

John Paul II. "XXV Anniversary of the Pontificate: Homily of His Holiness John Paul II." *The Holy See—The Holy Father—John Paul II.* October 16, 2003. http://www.vatican.va/holy _father/john_paul_ii/homilies/2003/documents/hf_jp-ii _hom_20031016_xxv-pontificate_en.html (July 5, 2004).

———. *Crossing the Threshold of Hope*. Translated by Jenny McPhee and Martha McPhee. New York: Alfred A. Knopf, 1994.

———. *Gift and Mystery*. New York: Doubleday, 1996.

———. *In My Own Words*. Liguori, MO: Liguori, 1998.

Levi, Virgilio, and Christine Allison. *John Paul II: A Tribute in Words and Pictures*. New York: William Morrow & Co., 1999.

O'Brien, Darcy. *The Hidden Pope: The Untold Story of a Lifelong Friendship That Is Changing the Relationship between Catholics and Jews: The Personal Journey of John Paul II and Jerzy Kluger*. New York: Daybreak Books, 1998.

O'Gorman, Bob, and Mary Faulkner. *The Complete Idiots Guide to Understanding Catholicism*. Indianapolis: Macmillan USA, 2000.

Szulc, Tad. *Pope John Paul II: The Biography*. New York: Scribner, 1995.

Valpy, Michael. "World Youth Day." *globeandmail.com*. July 20, 2002. http://www.globeandmail.com/special/wyd/stories/focus01 .html (June 24, 2004).

Weigel, George. *Witness to Hope: The Biography of Pope John Paul II*. New York: HarperCollins, 1999.

FURTHER READING/WEBSITES

Adams, Simon. *World War II*. New York: Dorling Kindersley Publishing, 2004.

John Paul II. *Abba Pater*. CD-ROM, Sony. 1999.

———. *My Dear Young Friends: Pope John Paul II Speaks to Teens on Life, Love, and Courage*. Winona, MN: Saint Mary's Press, 2001.

Klein, Richard A., and Virginia D. Klein, eds. *Dear Papa: Children Celebrate Pope John Paul II, with Letters of Love and Affection*. Liguori, MO: Liguori/Triumph, 2003.

Oertelt, Henry, and Stephanie Oertelt Samuels. *An Unbroken Chain: My Journey through the Nazi Holocaust*. Minneapolis: Lerner Publications Company, 2000.

Pagot, Toni, and Sergio Toppi. *Pope John Paul II Comic Book*. Boston: Pauline Books and Media, 2002.

Whitney, Helen. *John Paul II: Millennial Pope*. VHS. Burbank, CA: Warner Home Video, 1999.

Zeinert, Karen. *The Warsaw Ghetto Uprising*. Brookfield, CT: Millbrook Press, 1993.

Zuehlke, Jeffrey. *Poland in Pictures*. Minneapolis: Twenty-First Century Books, 2006.

INDEX

OTHER TITLES FROM LERNER AND A&E®:

Arnold Schwarzenegger
Ariel Sharon
Arthur Ashe
The Beatles
Benito Mussolini
Benjamin Franklin
Bill Gates
Bruce Lee
Carl Sagan
Chief Crazy Horse
Christopher Reeve
Colin Powell
Daring Pirate Women
Edgar Allan Poe
Eleanor Roosevelt
Fidel Castro
Frank Gehry
George Lucas
George W. Bush
Gloria Estefan
Hillary Rodham Clinton
Jack London
Jacques Cousteau
Jane Austen
Jesse Owens
Jesse Ventura
Jimi Hendrix
J. K. Rowling
John Glenn

Latin Sensations
Legends of Dracula
Legends of Santa Claus
Louisa May Alcott
Madeleine Albright
Malcolm X
Mark Twain
Maya Angelou
Mohandas Gandhi
Mother Teresa
Nelson Mandela
Oprah Winfrey
Osama bin Laden
Princess Diana
Queen Cleopatra
Queen Elizabeth I
Queen Latifah
Rosie O'Donnell
Saddam Hussein
Saint Joan of Arc
Thurgood Marshall
Tiger Woods
Tony Blair
Vladimir Putin
William Shakespeare
Wilma Rudolph
Women in Space
Women of the Wild West
Yasser Arafat

ABOUT THE AUTHOR

Alison Behnke is an author and editor of children's books. As a little girl, she spent three years living in Rome, where she heard Pope John Paul II deliver the Christmas Eve Mass twice. She also attended one of the pope's weekly audiences in Saint Peter's Square with her Girl Scout troop and once heard him deliver his Easter address from the balcony above the square. She still enjoys traveling and learning about world history. Her other books include *Millard Fillmore, Italians in America, Italy in Pictures*, and *Afghanistan in Pictures*.